Single – For Now

*A Real-Life Look at God's Plan for Singles
Who Don't Plan to Stay Single*

By Tammy Sevcov

Editor, Kim Curtis
Cover Design, Aaron Clay

xulon
PRESS

Table of Contents

Forward

*M*y wife, Kimberly, and I had just arrived in Anaheim, California, to start our first church when we met Tammy Sevcov. She was very respectful, but far from shy; and focused, yet always making things fun. I realized quickly that there was something quite special about this teenage Bible college student. However, what I didn't know in September 1999 was that Tammy was actually a gift from God to help us prepare, launch and lead a powerful and fast-growing church.

Being a pastor, I am resolved that people must be supernaturally transformed by the teachings they hear. For this reason, I am very particular about who instructs the five levels of our discipleship classes. They must be genuine, anointed, gifted, skilled, doctrinally precise and funny. Tammy has been my number one choice to teach Level One for years. Why? Because in Level One we have students from almost the entire spectrum: Drug addicts to mature believers, and high school dropouts to PhDs from major universities and seminaries. This requires someone who can articulate both sound biblical exegesis and deeply impact the heart of the person who's never been to church—simultaneously in the same message. That's Tammy. I so trust her doctrinal precision and communicative grace that I would recommend her to teach anywhere.

Over the years I've seen many opportunities for Tammy to end her "single status" and venture into marriage with a godly man. Yet somehow she has always known that only meeting the basic biblical standard of simply being "equally yoked" would cause her to fall short of God's best for her and her ministry. Tammy's explanation of "Arranged Marriages" is as clear and solid as I've ever heard or read. This insight comes from her yearning to understand God's ways, and from the experience of learning to trust Him when her emotions were attempting to take control.

Though I wish I could say Tammy is simply a product of our ministry, which certainly could make our church look good, would overlook two important early influences: Her godly parents and God's evident calling on her life. Hard working, honest and a sincere love for God characterize the lives of Dema and George Sevcov. There is no doubt where Tammy's quest for truth began. Though like all of us, she's had many influences, God's grace on Tammy demands acknowledgement. He has given her an unusually bright mind to study, grasp and teach His Word in very relevant and practical ways. Her humility and relentless pursuit of truth motivates her to discover nuggets of wisdom that help us live the lives most people only dream of.

"Single—For Now" is my new favorite book, and I'm not even single! As I read it for the first time, I fought back tears on numerous occasions because it reminded me of the feelings and fears that tried to torment me as a young man, and how faithful God was to bless me with Kimberly, the desire of my heart (Psalm 37:4). I asked my children, ages 21 and 18, to read this book, and told them that other than the Bible, I've never seen more accurately compiled wisdom on how to please the Lord as a single person and to prepare for a great marriage. I'm convinced that "doing singlehood well" is an often overlooked yet vital key to a great marriage. I especially appreciate subjects Tammy addresses such as healthy boundaries, keys to staying safe and Satan's tactics. I am asking every single person in our church to read this book.

It's difficult to put into words the privilege, joy and irony of writing a foreword for an author who, more than anyone else to date, has helped put my own writings into print. Not only do I recommend this book very highly; I would stake my reputation on the character and competence of the author.

You're going to be so glad you read this!

Jerry Dirmann
Senior Pastor, The Rock
www.gototherock.com

Dedication

To the One who has changed me, helped me, led me
and put up with me too. You're not just My God,
You are truly everything to me and I love You.

To my parents, who intentionally chose to seek
God's will and showed those who watched
that it is the best way to live.

And to my pastors—and now my friends—Jerry and Kimberly,
you will never know the full impact you've had on me,
but I thank you for being who you are. This book
literally would never have happened without you.

Preface

*B*eing single is not a disease that needs a cure.

It is not a limitation or handicap on a person's calling and purpose.

Not having a spouse does not make you more or less capable, attractive or content.

However, it can be, and has been, the cause for both internal frustration as well as license to receive unwanted advice for centuries.

Many ministers wax eloquently on the virtues of marriage, finding a good spouse and even the importance of raising a godly family . . . but what about those of us who aren't in that season? Whether "not yet" or you find yourself "back there again," what does God's Word say about being single—when you don't plan to stay that way?

The following pages are the result of neither study nor theory alone. This is the life I've lived, the struggles I've faced and the reality of the God I serve, which has culminated in the truths contained herein. Circumstances can be a tricky teacher and experience can be deceptive. However, when we take a look at God's Word, we have the opportunity to see the reality of both whom He is and who we are supposed to be.

That, my friends, is the ultimate reality.

And along with my own brand of sarcastic wit (which I hope you'll both understand and enjoy along the way), it is what I've accumulated in this little book.

I pray you don't read this and like it—but that you're forever impacted to live life to the full—and make your priority in everything Jesus.

Introduction

*I*f I could give you just one piece of advice as a single person, it would be this: "Don't follow your heart."

Are you shocked? Maybe a little bothered by that statement?

You might be saying, "What do you mean DON'T follow my heart? Do you mean I *shouldn't* be happy? I shouldn't *enjoy* life?" Actually, I mean just the opposite. My hope is that you discover true happiness, true joy. I want your life to be so much more than what your own heart will ever give to you. I want you to discover the fullness of what God created you to be, and to one day marry the person that will complement and release you into all the Lord has for you.

Here is the rub *(as they say)*: The Holy Spirit gives us an important insight in the Book of Jeremiah that most people ignore. It says, *"The heart is deceitful above all things, and desperately wicked; who can know it? (Jeremiah 17:9)* So, although people constantly say to "listen to your heart" or "follow your heart," what they don't understand is that your heart is not always the source of God's direction.

You see, our hearts are infected; they aren't pure. Yes, Jesus can speak through our heart, but so does our "natural man," the flesh part of us. That part doesn't want what's *best* for us; it wants what *seems to satisfy*. But isn't it true that in the pursuit of pleasure, being satisfied is a black hole of bondage? Lust. Greed. Thirst. Partaking doesn't satiate them; they only increase. This is how addictions are born. We simply cannot cure this impurity by trying to satisfy ourselves with what our heart wants. It's going to take something bigger than us.

Since the Garden of Eden, Satan has been spinning the same lies, showing off something that "looks good" to get us to take a bite; even when God has given us clear instruction to the contrary. Still, somehow, we fall for his tricks. We take a bite . . . and sometimes, we don't stop at one. We chew, we swallow and we go back for more, convinced that this is bringing us that desirable outcome we were promised. All the while, we're being evicted from the good life God set up for us to enjoy; and now we're moving out of the garden altogether.

Singles, please believe me when I tell you . . . in fact, I implore you: Do **not** follow your heart. Follow the Lord.

SECTION ONE

Why Are We Longing for Marriage Anyway?

*I*f you've been a Christian for long, you know that from the pulpit to the sweet little ladies in the pews, marriage is expected of you. You *will* get married. I'm not saying this as a doctrinal fact, but as a reality of life in the church world. If you've been single for long (you know, if you're over 19 years old) you've been greeted, "Have you met anyone yet?" as a not-so-gentle reminder that you ought to be getting married. In fact, if you're over 22, people may start wondering if you're one of those who are "called" to be single, or (as one "spiritual gifts" test put it) you have the "gift of celibacy." Ha! Someone needs to re-read a few passages of Scripture on that one . . . but I digress.

Regardless of everyone else's perspective, the truth in your own heart is likely that you *do* want to be married—whether you're 19, 39 or 59. You have a desire in your heart to find that like-minded mate with whom you will grow old. Since the title of this chapter may have misled you, let me clarify: Wanting marriage is not a bad thing! Hey, God created marriage. Right? It's funny though how we go from knowing God created it to figuring out how to accomplish it on our own. Due to my own amusement with human nature, one of my favorite things to hear is a single person stating they're "ready" for marriage. Like there's any chance that you are so knowledgeable as to determine when you are prime for marriage-ability? *You've watched your own life, determined that you've adequately grown and now,* thus saith you, *"I'm ready!" Sounds a little presumptuous, don't you think?*

The fact is, we're living this life trying to do the best we can, hoping and praying that somehow God will help us along the way to find that "right person" so we, too, can join the ranks of the Married Group. Indulge yourself and me for a moment: Can we just ask the question, "Why?" What is it that drives us forward toward that as our goal? I'm not saying it's bad, I'm just asking the question. What is it about being single that has come to be equated with being unhappy or unfulfilled? *Yet, it certainly has.* I've been asked on more than one occasion about my marriage prospects to have it followed by *"you know I just want you to be happy."* I want to tilt my head and perk an ear like a confused puppy, *"Huh? Do I seem UN-happy? Do I look depressed?"* I don't understand how it is that my being single somehow demands lack of joy . . . I thought I was doing well. Maybe I'm unhappy and I didn't realize it.

Unfortunately there is a huge demographic of singles that would consider themselves unhappy and relate that fact back to their marital status. In fact, this may describe you. I believe God has something so much better for us. A life that's not only fulfilling now, but will be even more blessed than most after we make that trek down the aisle (or stand at the end of it as the case may be).

We all want that special day to come *(some have planned and prepared for it in such detail that you wouldn't know they weren't already engaged . . . but again, I digress).* We want to experience that beautiful progression from meeting to marriage. It's that journey from *knowing* to *intimacy.* We hope that the next one might just be *"the one."* So we pray and we look and we wonder, and we long for the voyage that we've watched others take— from encounter to enchanted, from enchanted to enamored, from enamored to in love, from in love to *one flesh.* Then, of course the next progression begins. From in love to aware, from aware to annoyed, from annoyed to unhappy and from unhappy to marriage counseling. *I know, I know, I sound like a bitter old lady . . .* but let's be realistic for a few moments. If you've been around married couples much at all, you can acknowledge that this digression is very "normal." Sometimes it's quick, other times it takes awhile; but regardless, the glimmer starts to fade, and reality of living with another human that doesn't do things like you sets in. I remember hearing a newlywed at church talking to other people about their irritation with their new spouse about some habit that irked them each morning. *This* was in the first year of marriage when they supposedly can do no wrong! Why on earth are you talking to your buddies like marriage is already a hardship? C'mon! Aren't you still infatuated? *Did it really wear off that quickly?*

In a word: Yes.

But it is reality. You can't walk around googly-eyed forever, can you? Like they say, "The real work starts after the wedding." You've got to "make it work." Somewhere in the back of our minds we do know this. We recognize that it won't be all roses. We understand that we will put up with the issues because of the power of partnership. We tolerate the disappointments because at least we're no longer alone. We bear up under the additional burdens so that we can simply BE married. We DO know it happens, but for some reason, singles don't actually think it will happen to them.

I've watched it time and again. What was meant to be so good and so blessed becomes simply bewildering as these two people attempt to unify their very different lives and perspectives. Newly married people are stunned that there's so much to deal with! They're amazed that the solution they thought they were getting wasn't so much of a solution. In fact, in the last 12 years of ministry, I've discovered a startling reality: Most of the loneliest people I talk to are married. Hear me, this isn't always because they're in a "bad" marriage either. However, a little too late, they discovered that marriage is not the cure-all that we've been told it is. When people say, "I just want you to be happy," it ought to be so effortless to respond with, "I am!" Yet, this begs another question: If I'm not happy, "why" am I not happy? Being without a spouse should not answer that question. However, until we understand what marriage is not, and what we are not, we will still keep thinking our joy is wrapped up and waiting at the altar.

It's simple, really. We have a certain list of things we don't like about being single that marriage is *guaranteed* to answer (or so we think):

- I'm scared of the unknown and I want a partner to help me face the future.
- I'm lonely and want to come home to *someone*.
- I don't feel whole. I want that "other half" I'm missing.
- I need to be married or I will keep falling into physical temptations and sin.
- I don't feel like I can handle the financial burdens of life and marriage would give some financial security.
- I just want to feel stable.

You may be able to pick out a few of these for yourself off the bat. You can quickly identify with one or more that speaks to your perspective. Maybe there are a few others you can think of. We all have areas that we assume marriage will fix just by the nature of the partnership it brings. **The unfortunate reality is that none of these are simply answered by saying "I do."**

Consider this: Marriage brings another person with their issues into the mix. Suddenly another person's life is intricately involved in yours. To top it off, the very thing we believe will solve our own issues creates a new list of them. I promise, I'm not someone who hates marriage. I, too, want to meet that perfect mate, but I believe that in order to find the right person, there's more to my part than *wishing* and *hoping* and *thinking* and *praying* . . . it's going to take some vision and direction and clarity *from the Lord* to do this right.

What Does God Say About Marriage?

Did you ever stop to think about how God set this system up? I've already stated that God created marriage. So obviously He knew what **He** was doing (*we on the other hand . . . well, you know*). If you take a moment to consider the realties of what marriage actually means, you'll quickly see why it's a challenge! Let me paint a picture for you:

> Two people of different genders (chemical makeup, hormonal balance), from different backgrounds (family, culture, etc.), having varying life experiences (age, height, weight, looks, social standing) and beliefs (from doctrinal nuances to experiential belief systems) come together to become *one flesh.* These two individual lives are supposed to be joined into a unity of unconditional love and harmony—*for the rest of their lives.*

What was God thinking?

We could stop right here and probably answer a lot of "why" questions when it comes to divorce and dysfunctional families! Yet, God did create it. He ordained marriage. Which means He created it to work . . . and to work well! I repeat, God knew what **He** was doing; but us? *Not so much.* Just look at the state of marriage in our society. You will quickly get a glimpse, NOT of God's original design, but instead what the fall of mankind has done. We see the results of Adam's and Eve's decision in every broken home, in every fighting couple, in every abandoned child. We see a society that doesn't mirror God's plan and we can be lulled into accepting those realities as our own fate as well.

One of my biggest pet peeves is hearing Christians say, "I'm only human." You may think that's odd. After all, we do make mistakes and we are not God. *True.* However, I'm convinced that in the midst of this statement of "fact" is hidden a relinquishing of our very mandate by God. IF Jesus Christ is our Savior and Lord, aren't we changed? Aren't we more than merely another person swayed by this world? If we've invited the Holy Spirit to dwell within us, then our reality should be more *super*natural than natural. We now walk in the redeemed state that mankind was originally intended to operate in. Now we are not just *us*, we have *Christ in us*. **That's a big deal.**

So what does that mean for marriage? Should I expect anything different than what society has to offer for my own marriage?

After all, *the church is filled with people who are doing things the way the world does them. It seems like that's just the way it is nowadays.* Well, that may be their reality, but yours is yet to be determined. **Do you want better than what's typical? Do you desire a life and a marriage that's beyond the norm?** Dare I say, "incredible?" Rule Number One: If you want something to work differently, then you have to do things differently. Different actions equal different results. For some reason, we just think *wishin' and hopin'* will equate to different results. Better results mean a better direction and better information. That demands tapping into the Divine reality of God's plan for our life and our marriage.

So, we look back at the beginning to see how God set this whole thing up at the outset. We look back to the garden, the origination of mankind as well as marriage.

> *Then God said, "Let us make man in Our image, according to Our likeness and let them have dominion . . ." So God created man in His own image; in the image of God He created him; male and female He created them." (Genesis 1:26–27)*

> *And the Lord God said, "It is not good that man should be alone . . ." (Genesis 2:18)*

When God created humanity he created us male and female. Mankind is two parts. We aren't complete without each other. HUMANITY needs both men and women functioning together to properly reflect the image of God. In fact, our mandate was to be together, to have joint dominion over the earth, to be a cooperating, unified leadership team. Unfortunately, instead of seeing the design set forth at creation as the template for humankind, it has somehow come to mean that individuals are not whole without a marriage partner. *That's simply not true.* When we were born, we had all the necessary pieces to be a whole person. We can function without another human attached to us. We are fully capable of creating, inventing, developing; and the list goes on. We recognize that as humans, however, we will never function well without others because we're designed to *connect.*

Marriage is not the source of all human connectedness. The idea that someone is to be our "other half" gives the picture that we're only half a person. I cannot imagine Jesus looking at any of us and saying, "Good job . . . for a *halfer*! Just wait till you get married, then I can really use you!" Jesus isn't waiting for us to get married . . . **so why are we?** Let me paint this picture a little clearer: When Jesus takes us home to heaven there will be no marriage. (Matthew 22:30) He didn't seem to think that was critical for our afterlife. I wonder why we can feel like it's hamstringing our current life?

I have an idea where this thinking comes from. Consider the average church. You'll see men's groups and women's groups and then separate groups for singles and those who are married. We put everyone in their space to help them make like-minded friends and address journey-specific issues. It makes great sense, but we do it to the point that we can lose the image of a unified mankind—together leading—together reflecting God's image. I'm not saying that these groupings are *causing* a distorted picture, but it seems that they can reinforce a wrong worldview. The only time we see men and women functioning together are as married couple units. A segregated picture of humanity has kind of become the norm. It's no wonder that the ugliness of racism was once acceptable in church. We're so used to dividing everyone, it's just another point of keeping us separate "for our own benefit."

The body of Christ is fractured and divided and that's not helping anyone. There are doctrinal divides, styles of worship to divide us, even churches who are so busy fighting with other churches that we've forgotten who the real fight is against. We seem to like division and that's dangerous. The Lord warned us that every "house divided against itself cannot stand." (Matthew 12:25) I wonder where all these divisions are really coming from? If I were Satan, that would be one of my primary focuses. After all, it's guaranteed to bring down the house.

The Church itself often sends mixed signals to men and women. Strong women are asked to lead, but then also told to be more quiet or passive. Quiet men who may function more creatively are lauded for their talents while also being told to 'man up' or fulfill some picture of true masculinity. Why are we trying so hard to make people be a certain way? Isn't Jesus looking at our hearts? Can we accept each other's differences and learn to work together? If we can't seem to get on the same page about how God created us as PEOPLE, it's not surprising that we're unclear on how God has deemed marriage to work!

If we want to see how God set things up for marriage, we have to look again before the fall of mankind, as God brings the woman to Adam. There's not nearly as much information in those first two chapters of the Bible as I would have liked, but there's enough to see that God's intention for the world was vastly different than the reality in which we live. If we want to reflect the picture of God's redeemed people, we need to recognize not just what we were redeemed from, **but what He was returning us to**.

> *And the Lord God said, "It is not good that man should be alone; I will make him a helper comparable to him." And Adam said: "This is now bone of my bones and flesh of my flesh; She shall be called Woman because she was taken out of man." Therefore the Man shall leave his father and mother and be joined to his wife, and they shall become one flesh. And they were both naked and were not ashamed." (Genesis 2:18, 23–25)*

This is the picture we long for. The Hebrew language used here is a picture of a perfect counterpart. Don't let the word "helper" mess with your thinking. This is the same word that's used to describe God as our "help." This isn't the image of someone who runs errands, but the missing piece that completes the plan. In essence this is the piece that rescues the whole. Finally, creation was complete. Then the Holy Spirit commentates on this picture, clarifying that it's because of this good union and what it was meant to be that a man will leave that which he's known as his family and start a new life as a unit with the woman. This is the precious approach that the Lord created for us. To compliment one another as we're joined together, "forsaking all others" to belong to each other.

Then comes the most incredible comment: *They were both naked and not ashamed.* What's packed into that statement has been so trivialized. We just read over it and attribute the commentary to some recognition of their naiveté or sinless innocence, instead of looking to see why the Holy Spirit made sure to include those words. Why is it important that we, God's redeemed people, understand what it was like before man's fall? We have to see how God set up the system to work in the first place. Consider this: Man and woman standing there completely unclothed and not even the slightest bit awkward. The truth of that freedom has to do with the sanctity of the garden. You see, in the Garden of Eden there was no chance for abuse. No potential for violation. There was only wholeness and acceptance. There was only trust and connectedness to both God and each other. The garden, at this point, was safe. He wouldn't injure her. She wouldn't violate him. He wouldn't judge her. She wouldn't undermine him. There was a unity and a like-mindedness that eliminated all possible fear or concern. It was sin that changed that. It is Jesus who redeemed us back. **This is the picture of what marriage is meant to be.**

I know some readers at this point are starting to wonder if I could really be serious. *THIS is the picture of marriage we're supposed to plan for? I can hardly imagine getting to that place by myself, never mind involving another human's will!* Did you ever notice that God doesn't talk like we do? Even about OUR lives. He speaks very boldly, very expectantly . . . very emphatically that we have huge potential. Read through these few verses:

- *"And God is able to make ALL grace abound toward you, that you, always having ALL sufficiency in ALL things, may have an ABUNDANCE for every good work." (2 Corinthians 9:8)*
- *"And my God shall supply ALL your needs according to His RICHES in glory by Christ Jesus." (Philippians 4:19)*
- *"The Lord is my Shepherd I SHALL NOT want . . ."* (Psalm 23:1)
- *"The Lord is my light and my salvation whom shall I fear? The Lord is the strength of my life . . ." (Psalm 27:1)*

- *"What then shall we say to these things? If God is for us, who can be against us? He who did not spare His own Son, but delivered Him up for us all, how shall He not with Him also freely give us all things?" (Romans 8:31, 32)*
- *". . . if we ask ANYTHING according to His will, He hears us and if we know He hears us, we KNOW we HAVE the petitions that we have asked of Him." (John 5:14–15)*
- *"For by You I can run against a troop, by my God I can leap over a wall." (Psalm 18:29)*
- *"Ask, and it will be given to you; seek, and you will find; knock, and it will be opened to you. For everyone who asks receives, and he who seeks finds, and to him who knocks it will be opened." (Matthew 7:7, 8)*

Now, in those few words from Scripture, do you notice that God doesn't seem to talk about our life the way we do? You see, it's not just regarding marriage that we should be thinking differently, it's in every area of our lives. You may argue, *"But I haven't seen all of these Scriptures to be reality in my life, so how can I talk like that?"* Do you remember when the psalmist said, *"Let the weak SAY, I am strong, let the poor SAY I am rich?"* Or when David declared in Psalm 91, *"I will SAY of the Lord He is my refuge, and my fortress, my God in whom I will trust . . ."*?

There's something about believing and accepting God's Word before we see the reality of it come to pass that honors the Lord and makes room for His Divine guidance. What would happen if we would really take God at His Word? Could we actually live like He says? God doesn't change His mind, but we've certainly been unclear on what we really believe of Him. He is trying to get our attention, to help us see who He is calling us to be. To allow our minds to grasp what life in Him is MEANT to be, not just what we've thought it is.

It's along with these verses that speak with clarity to His purpose for our lives that two more Scriptures come to mind on this topic:

- *"He who finds a wife finds a good thing and obtains favor from the Lord." (Proverbs 18:22)*

- *". . . no good thing will He withhold from those who walk uprightly." (Psalm 87:11b)*

God wants you to have the marriage that's a GOOD THING. He desires that we not only get married (if that desire is in us), but that we have a life-long enjoyable relationship. He's just THAT good! This is the vision we need to catch; the new reality we need to see. In God's mind, marriage is not what we've seen played out in society, but a picture we need to paint **from His Word.**

In the book of Proverbs (29:18) it says, *"Where there is no revelation* (vision, divine communication) *the people cast of restraint* (don't hold back, ignore caution)." Our culture has cast off restraint. Few seem to be cautious anymore about living life according to God's standards. Just as this proverb declares, it is because they don't have the revelation or understanding of what God has said. Oh, they may "know" what God said, but they don't "get it." Sometimes the Church has preached AT people what God says is true, forgetting that those whom they are talking at have no reason to accept God's truth as a good thing. Why would someone live according to God's standards when they do not see the point of it? After all, even the Bible states that sin is pleasurable for a time. (Hebrews 11:25) So why not just enjoy what you can, while you can? If a person doesn't catch the vision, understanding a true revelation of God's goodness, then satisfying self is all there is to live for, and so, they do.

As God's children we can do the same thing. Oh, we may have rules or guidelines about certain aspects of our behavior, but I'm talking about having a genuine vision of how God wants our marriages to be and how it IS attainable! God wants to paint this picture for us. He wants us to capture a vision in our own hearts to see marriage from His perspective. The revelation we *should* have, the picture we're missing, starts back in the garden.

No more are we going to "hope for the best" when it comes to our life-long commitment to another human. Instead, we must expect the best. We will EXPECT that God is with us, He is for us and He has good things in store. It's time for us to understand how to pursue THAT vision.

Who Is In Charge?

I called this book "Single—*For Now*" because as a life-long church attendee I'd heard a lot about being married, and even some about living single as a life-choice. However, I found that rarely was anyone teaching on living single when a person doesn't plan to stay that way. I want to obey and honor God, to fulfill His plan for my life, but if "my life" doesn't begin until I'm married (as many seem to indicate), then there's a lot of random junk that's sure to fill my time until then. That just didn't seem right. When I spoke to other singles however, they always talked about their future in conjunction with a spouse . . . a spouse I'll remind you that didn't yet exist. It's like their future was wrapped in a wedding. Once they got there, they'd get to start living. When it's stated like that, no one would *agree* that they believe that, but consider how so many have approached life . . . you might have to admit this has affected your thinking too.

This means we need to hear God's Word on our singleness as well as how to direct our lives the best way toward marriage. That's what I believe the Lord wants to do in you as you go through this book.

When we're going to address any area of life fulfillment there is one question that must be answered first: Who is in charge? The world trains us that we are the masters of our own destiny. When we give our life to Jesus, inviting Him to be our Savior, accepting His payment for our sins, we enter into a covenant—a binding relationship—wherein we make Him "Lord." We don't use the term "Lord" in our present-day cultures very often, but an easy definition of the word is "master." We accept that we could have never paid for our own sins and we take His payment on our behalf. Thereby agreeing to the terms of that exchange. We take on His life, as He took on ours at the cross.

> *"I have been crucified with Christ; **it is no longer I who live**, but Christ that lives in me; and the life which I live in the flesh I live by faith in the Son of God, who loved me and gave Himself for me." (Galatians 2:20)*

When you trade in your ugly sinfulness, you agree that your life is gone. Dead. From then on, your life is His. **He is Lord.** You take the baton He passed when He was crucified, to fulfill His assignment on the earth. *Now, I'm not going to get weird and tell you that since Jesus never married, we're not supposed to either.* However, by accepting His death as ours, our right to make that decision on our own also died with Him. We traded. The choice of whom we marry now rightfully belongs to our Lord. The **very** good thing about that is He's a whole lot smarter than we are *(really, He is, if you don't know that—well, I suppose that proves my point)*. Not only that, but He wants that marriage to be incredible, even more than we do. So this really isn't a scary thought, but it is another layer of acknowledging His Lordship over our life. The sooner we catch this truth, the less fighting we'll do with God.

So when He says in Psalm 84:11, ". . . *no good thing will He withhold from those who walk uprightly,*" He IS saying that He DOES withhold things that are not good. He made this so real to me years ago when I was praying about a certain guy I was spending time with. I was feeling frustrated because I couldn't get any sense of peace in my spirit about allowing a relationship to develop with him. My flesh wanted to allow something more to develop. After all he was a good guy who loved God. We were already good friends, but the reality was that I was too aware of the Lordship of Jesus in my life by that time that I simply couldn't permit something that I wasn't sure He was pleased with. In the middle of a worship service, that (Psalm 84:11) is the verse He gave me. I had one of those teary moments with the Lord, recognizing that if He's withholding something (or in this case, someone) from me, it's because that something or someone *isn't good for me.* He may be good, but not for me. I repented of my selfishness, and have never regretted releasing that "brother" from my life. I'm too convinced God's plan for me is always best.

I've heard it said there are three types of people in the world: (1) Those that make things happen; (2) Those that watch things happen; and (3) Those that say, "what happened?" There is such truth to that statement. If we don't pay careful attention, life can happen *to* us. Yet, when we were created in God's image, the picture was not of passive creatures that were like the cattle and birds, but instead like God, those who had choice and under-standing. It's our purpose that makes us different. Life should happen **through** us.

It's up to us to take hold of that destiny. Often, without our conscious consent we can start walking down a path we wouldn't have intentionally chosen. Unfortunately, by the time we notice, it can seem like it's "too late." You may not think this applies to you because you believe you make good choices and you're a good person. Or maybe you know exactly what I'm talking about and you already feel like things are too far-gone. The truth is that we all need a bit of a reality check. First, consider this: Think of those you might call "evil" or "bad" people. Take it to an extreme: Mass murderers, rapists or even home wreckers. Do you think that as a child these individuals aimed to become evil? So, do we excuse their behavior due to the circumstances that led them there? Certainly not! However, is any one of them beyond God's redemption? Absolutely not! It's never too late to turn.

What about those of us who "do good?" Is *that* the prereq-uisite to fulfilling our destiny? Have you read the Bible? There is a lot more than "being a nice person" to our walk of faith. Just take a look at the book of Acts. Is the image of the early church "nice people" or something that's powerful and incredible? Being stuck in "nice Christian mode" simply perpetuates the typical church culture that's been around for years; something like, "*nice people, with okay lives.*" Sure, there are exceptions, both to the positive and the negative. However, in my experience the reality of Christianity in North America is pretty mediocre. I am simply too aware of what Scripture lays out to settle for that in my own life. **Jesus didn't pay the ultimate price so I could be a nice person.** He certainly didn't hand me His baton of ministry so I could live like everyone else on the earth. It's time that the people of God step up and refuse to take less than the supernatural results God wants to show through us. Let me clarify, however, **this will demand that we die to self and become wholly dependent on Him.**

Choosing that path means making new kinds of choices. Where we are today is a summation of the choices we've made so far. The sometimes-unfortunate reality is that many choices were made for us. Other people, maybe parents or home situations have greatly impacted where we are today. Regardless, it's been a series of choices that's got us to today, and that is what will take us forward from here to the next destination. That destination can either be intentional or it can be by happenstance, depending on how *we* choose. Today, there is a choice within our grasp. Today we have opportunity to make new choices, to change direction or adjust our course. Time will keep passing and life will keep going . . . *do you know where you're headed?*

There's no getting around it. We have to make right choices for things to work God's way. It doesn't naturally just *happen*. Adam and Eve made just one, *really bad decision (seriously, could we just avoid that tree? Maybe build a giant fence or something so we don't get stupid one day?).* Their one really bad decision altered their lives. It altered humanity forever. I always wonder what difference might have been made had they repented. I believe at least their kids would have been impacted differently. But we'll never know. No, they messed up and had to deal with the consequences for the rest of their lives. In fact, we have to deal with their consequences too . . . all because of choices.

We often mistakenly believe that whatever God wants for our lives will work automatically. It's some automated system that when we commit our lives to Jesus, He runs things from then on. *I wish!* The Bible makes it pretty clear that although God is sovereign, and the end result is already determined, that doesn't mean He controls everyone. In fact, there are a lot of things that He wants to happen that don't (2 Peter 3:9). Just take a look at the children of Israel as they circled the desert. They had to live with the consequences when they continued to resist God's will (hint: *it didn't go well for them*), even though He made it plain. We also must live with the consequences if we continue to resist His will. It's our choices that either align us to His will and plan, or which we refuse.

This is where a lot of Believers miss it. They never seem to see God's goodness in their lives like the Bible talks about. They may have given God a new title (Lord), but there's been no follow through. Can you imagine getting hired for a new job, telling everyone whom your new "boss" is, but never showing up for work? I would like to observe that conversation the day you arrive to collect a paycheck anyway. You'd quickly discover that just calling him or her your boss wasn't the key to what you were hoping for. Similarly, calling Jesus Lord is not the key to walking out His purpose for our life.

Simply said, we are not on autopilot. Unfortunately a lot of Christians think that's the way it works. Somehow our understanding of God's sovereignty has deteriorated into a fatalistic view of life. We're just like the world, blaming things on fate; but instead we blame everything on God. Oh, it may seem like it's good, like He wanted these bad things to happen so it's actually *a blessing;* but when push comes to shove, there's a lot of passing the buck to take all responsibility off our own shoulders. We act as though we had no choice because it must have been God's will.

This life we live is one in which we have to be actively involved. Ephesians 2:10 states that the good works God planned for us, we **should** walk in. As in, we **ought to,** not that we will automatically fulfill. If we really want to *be* who God has designed us to be and to *do* what He has called us to do, we have a very active role to play.

Remember, there is also a real enemy, Satan. Do not be unaware. He has a plan for us too. If he gets his way (like he did with Adam and Eve), we'll walk away from God's plan completely. He does not play fair and he does not play nice. In fact, for him, this is no game at all. He will come in little by little, asking questions like, "Did God **really** say that you can't have that?" Or leading us with promises like, "But it's really good for you! You would like it." Until one day we look up to find we aren't even in the garden at all anymore. The lush vegetation has been traded for wilderness. The presence of God walking with us was traded in for that thing Satan promised to help us take hold of . . . that doesn't actually satisfy like we thought.

Did you ever consider that Satan promised Adam and Eve that they would be "like God" if they ate of the fruit? I've heard people talk about how Satan was so crafty to offer them something they could never have. Yet, the truth is startling as it's almost the opposite. Satan was promising *the very thing that they were cre-ated as.* God created us in HIS likeness and after HIS image. We were meant to be "like" Him! It's such a sad commentary on our humanity that the very thing God wants to show us how to fulfill is what we followed Satan to secure. We need to wake up to the fact that God's boundaries are for our protection not restriction. He wants to get us the good stuff, but He wants to be the source we get it from. He knows He's a better "Lord" than we or Satan will ever be. Now we need to get that through our heads!

We've all seen people who seem to be doing well, serving God, going to church, doing the right things. One day we look up and they're not around anymore. We discover they're far from the life they were leading; and heading down a destructive course, even opposing the things they used to profess. It's a startling reality and a stark reminder. Satan will lure and trick and deceive. Jesus said in John 10:10, *"The thief does not come except to steal and to kill and to destroy, but I have come that you may have life and that you may have it more abundantly."* Jesus makes it very clear where destruction comes from. He also presents a very important truth that we overlook. His desire is for us to have an abundant life. Going all the way back to the garden God's set-up was always for us to have that which is good and pleasing—but He wants us to get it the safe way—His way.

Surrendering Self

God's way will always start with surrender.

> *"I beseech you therefore by the mercies of God that you present your bodies a living sacrifice . . . and do not be conformed to this world, but be transformed by the renewing of your mind that you may prove what is that good and acceptable and perfect will of God."*
> *(Romans 12:1, 2)*

In the book of Romans, Paul exhorts us to present our bodies as *a living sacrifice* to God, giving our whole selves to Him. He follows that with this phrase, "That **you** may **PROVE** what is that . . . perfect will of God." Wait! Did you catch that? How do WE prove God's will? How do we make it so that what our life reflects is a perfect image of what He desires? Is that even possible? Well, the

Holy Spirit inspiring this passage seemed to think so. He is telling us that by presenting *our* whole self to Him, He now has the permission to work within us, in every way. By giving ourselves entirely to God, our life will begin to **be proof!**

So many people hear about Jesus or religion and they say they want proof. They want to know why they should believe. We turn to apologetics or feel like we need to know the Bible more in order to argue with them and prove God is true. Let me clarify that I wholeheartedly believe in the value of apologetics. Even more, I know that genuine Bible study is critical to our life in Jesus. Paul gave us something so much bigger to wrestle with. **We are supposed to be the proof!** The apostle Paul was making this call, not to unbelievers but to Believers. He was asking Christians to give themselves over to God. *Why?* Because this is not a one-time act of repentance, but a lifestyle of submitting to God that will create the evidence this world is longing for. In fact, it's the evidence that even the Church is looking for! If we continue to live for ourselves, there will only be spots and pieces of evidence to point toward that show God's reality. When we live our lives wholly surrendered to God, Paul says we will **prove** God's perfect will. It will shine through us. So where are these lives that prove His will? Moreover, where are these marriages that prove God's goodness to the fullest extent? Rest assured, there are some out there. *However, God is asking for more.* He's asking **us**, today, if we will let Him do a work in us. He wants us to allow our lives to be the proof others are looking for. To be a picture that the world can look to and know that it is possible to have one's life so enveloped by God that our marriage reflects His perfect will.

I wasn't always convinced of God's plan for my life. In fact, I was pretty sure I was alone. I was only about 16 when I hit bottom. I can't really say what triggered the downward spiral. I just knew I was done. I was tired of life and tired of living. I wanted out.

I was raised in a Christian home and at one point I'd asked my mother if those who committed suicide went to heaven. She answered that she didn't know for sure. I'm so glad she answered that way, as that ended up being my "saving grace" during that dark time. I truly wanted to deny there was a God, to take up Job's wife's mantra, "curse God and die," but the truth was that I had simply seen and known too much in my early years to be able to convince myself He really wasn't there. *I may not have been happy with God, but I couldn't deny His existence.* That didn't mean I wanted to live, it just meant that the looming possibility of hell remained and therefore kept me from choosing what my heart wanted: An end to this life. It was my own logic that I believe the Holy Spirit used to help me begin the climb out of that pit. My inner monologue went something like this. 'A miserable existence for another 60-some years on earth is better than an eternity burning in hell.' *Hey, I've never claimed genius status, but simple logic can help at times, especially when emotions are raging.* That same logical drive began to help me to the next step. 'Well, if God is real, then He created me. If He created me, then it wasn't to be miserable. There's got to be more to life than this.'

So it began. My trek from being raised a Christian toward finding what it was to know God, serve God and genuinely LOVE God in a personal way. I started making changes in my life *(again, simple logic prevailed; 'If how I've been living my life is leading to this outcome, then I need to do things differently.').* I didn't have a book I was following or a holy angel that instructed me. I simply started changing things. I tossed all my secular music *(well, that would actually be ALL of my music)* and asked a friend to make a mix of some of the Christian artists she listened to. I'll be honest, *that wasn't easy.* I wasn't a huge fan of what was popular at that time in the Christian recording industry. However, something inside me was more concerned with getting different results than listening to the music I wanted to. I started reading my Bible every day. It really didn't mean a whole lot to me. I wasn't reading for content, I was reaching out for a lifeline . . . for hope . . . for anything to help reverse those dark thoughts that loomed so constantly. I was just trying to do things differently. More like how God might want.

I wasn't having divine encounters in my bedroom. I was simply putting different content into my gray matter. I was hoping more than believing that something would happen. I also began to pray each night. I prayed out loud. *If God is real, I'm going to treat Him like a real person. I'm going to TALK to Him not just think toward Him.* However, I will clarify that I was 16 years old with a reputation to protect. I couldn't have my parents or siblings hearing me talking to God *(amazing how our minds work)*. So, I spoke out loud, but into a pillow, just in case.

Not once in these times of listening to Christian music, praying out loud *(into a pillow)* or reading my Bible did I sense God's holy presence or hear the angels of heaven respond. Not once did these times become what some might call an "encounter." I just had to stop living in this darkness that was surrounding me and "if God is real" then I was giving Him a chance to show up. It was maybe a month or two after I started this journey that I had a startling realization.

I was walking down my street all alone and I smiled to myself. I froze mid-stride. 'I smiled? Why? What was I thinking about that was happy?' You see it had been a very long time since I smiled for any other reason than as an act for those I was in the room with, *but I was alone*. I literally racked my brain trying to figure out what caused me to smile. It was just so bizarre. That's when I realized it: *I was just happy*. I mean, not bouncing off the walls happy, but the dark thoughts weren't looming. The frustration, hurt and bitterness weren't there. *Something* was very different. It wasn't like it had been. I suddenly realized I was feeling "good." I practically wanted to skip home *(and I may have, but I was 16 and had a reputation to protect)*!

It was around that age when I discovered the most incredible gift of my life. I had a relationship with a real God who really had a plan for my life. I gave myself into His hands and trusted that what He says is true, and it does work. I was changed. I have now become *proof* to people I minister to—to my friends and to my family—that God is who He said He is. When we obey, He DOES, in fact, come through. I no longer doubt not only His ability, but also His willingness to do great things in and through little ol' me. I am His workmanship, created in Christ Jesus.

So are you.

SECTION TWO

This Is Your Time

Paul gives a very strong exhortation to singles in the Corinthian church that I'd overlooked for years.

> *"But I want you to be without care* (worry). *He who is unmarried cares for the things of the Lord—how he may please the Lord. But he who is married cares about the things of the world—how he may please his wife. There is a difference between a wife and a virgin* (an unmarried woman). *The unmarried cares about the things of the Lord, that she may be holy both in body and spirit. But she who is married cares about the things of the world—how she may please her husband. And this I say for your own profit, not that I may put a leash on you, but for what is proper, and that you may serve the Lord without distraction." (1 Corinthians 7:32–35)*

When the Holy Spirit inspired this passage, He gave us incredible clarity on God's perspective of our single years. The foremost statement Paul makes is that the unmarried person "**cares for the things of the Lord.**" He says it like we should of course know that, because that is the way it is. If you're single, this is how it is. In fact, He clarifies this twice, once toward men, and again toward women. That's VERY uncommon in Scripture. Typically, we take for granted that almost any single passage is true for both genders. However, Paul (and the Lord) wanted to make sure we didn't miss this point: **Our single years do belong to Him.**

It is absolutely true (in general) that singles don't have the same "cares" that a married person does. So instead of filling our time with hobbies and pastimes, or even just TV and friends, God is calling singles to step up! There is no reason why single men and women of God can't be leading ministries, or even just participating a little more than our married counterparts. We shouldn't expect anything extra to be given *to us*, but *we ought to* be able to give a little (or a lot) more during this season. If we don't now, what do we think we'll do when the added pressures come along?

This is our time to seek Him, to know who He has called us to be. It's the most *time* we're ever going to have to fulfill Matthew 6:33 to, *"seek first the Kingdom of God and His righteousness . . ."* First comes the seeking of God. Then, He adds things to you. This season, this "right now" in your life is supposed to be all about Him.

Our dating culture flies in the face of this passage in 1 Corinthians. Instead of giving our single years to the Lord, we give them to a series of relationships that will eventually be broken. It's the entire intention of dating, that we fill our time, that we "try out" people to see what we like and we "fulfill our own life" through these relationships. Please don't hear a diatribe against dating per se. What I'm warning against is the form of what we've called "dating" *(yes, even in church)*. At best, this approach is dangerous. At worst it becomes idolatry. We replace finding our joy and contentment in the Lord with trying to find those things in a person. A person who becomes our filter for how we hear God, a person whose moods and personal struggles impact our own joy and confidence. Do you see why this thing we call "dating" can become a wedge in our relationship with God? It's not the "dating" that causes problems so much as what happens to our hearts. The pressure of what is expected by the other person and by our culture weighs on us.

While we're addressing this, there's another facet of dating we need to understand can cause major danger in the future. Dating is set up to help us discover our likes and dislikes, and to commit to a person until we get to a place where we either don't like the relationship anymore or we don't want to tolerate certain things about that person any longer. Whatever it is, there is, in essence, a threshold for when we will completely walk away, washing our hands of that person and situation. So, as single adults, we learn to invest time, energy and emotion into someone to the point it's no longer enjoyable or we don't feel like it benefits us the way we think it ought to, and then we walk away. We will do this maybe a few times, possibly a dozen or more and then, get married. Why are we surprised that people who "would never get divorced" are getting divorced? It's only rational that when they hit a certain threshold, it's time to walk away. We've been training ourselves this way for years! Unfortunately, when it comes to marriage, that tearing apart doesn't happen without long-lasting consequences.

When Paul cautioned us that these years are for the Lord, he clarified that this wasn't to be a leash, or a chain, but to simply recognize that these years are God's. This isn't about being shackled, but about understanding what is proper and right. The contrast he was pointing to was that once we're married, our time really does belong to our spouse. Of course, the problem we've just seen is that as a society we give our single years away too. What's left for the Lord? Maybe, our retired years are for Him? That may only work after our spouse dies. *Unfortunately, that only works for one of us.*

Once we are married, we will be married for the rest of our life. Try this: Remove the first 15 years of your life, as you grew toward adulthood, and count how many years since then you've been single (if you really want a better picture, count how many years you've been single and genuinely serving God). Now, consider your life span. Just to use a round number, let's say it will likely be 80 years. If you got married in 10 years, would you still have more *"life"* after marriage than before? The likely answer is yes. Many could wait to get married for another 25 years and still have significantly more life with their spouse than without. So why are we so anxious? It comes down to a deep-rooted belief that our spouse will somehow complete our lives, when the reality is that only Jesus can do that and only He was intended to.

Empowered and Enlightened Singles

Right now while we're single is the time the Lord is asking for. It's completely anti-culture. It doesn't even make sense to most people. They can't comprehend why we would do that. Of course, they're usually comparing our situation to their own, not to what God's Word says. I believe it's a new breed of Christians, who look a lot more like biblical disciples, who are willing to give up "everything else" to seek "whatever" the Lord asks of them.

We all need direction for our lives. We need to know what the Lord has called us to and in what ways He's uniquely gifted us to function in His body. That's not a single's thing, that's a human thing. However, most people don't take the time to do that. They don't set aside time to pursue their Creator to know His heart and mind for them. They simply keep living, and hoping it all turns out okay. Can you imagine what it might look like if singles were to be clear on their callings before they got married? What if young adults in our churches focused on hearing God's direction for their lives and pursued that instead of letting video games and movies steal these single years right out from under them? What if, when people got married, they were already engaged in the path God had called them to, instead of waiting to find it?

In my early 20s I noticed a startling trend. I felt like I was seeing more and more older singles (I'm not talking about elderly, but less people getting married right out of high school). I had put this before the Lord as a question, wondering if it *was* true and if so, why? Maybe it was just my perspective, but it seemed like good, godly singles who wanted to be married were just not "finding the one" or for whatever reason, not getting married. I was in a conversation with a friend who had gotten married right out of college. We were around the same age and she now had a few rambunctious little ones and was serving in a visible leadership capacity in ministry with her husband. It seemed like they had what most Christians would envy *(if we were allowed to envy, of course)*. As we spoke she opened up about how she was just starting to figure out her calling and find her "place" in ministry. I was stunned. I thought, 'How is it that she's been serving and living and being a mother and a wife, and six or more years later she's just "finding her place?'" It didn't seem right. She had such a lack of clarity even though she was doing all kinds of good things. She simply hadn't felt like she was in her "groove" and so much was going on, it was hard to figure out where that might be. As we stood there talking, I felt the Lord whisper in my ear. It was just as startling as her confession, but I heard *(not audibly, inside)* "I don't have time for that anymore." I immediately understood the fuller picture that He was alluding to. He was saying that time is short. This earth we live in won't be the same for long and He's asking His singles to get clear. He wants His people, and especially singles, to know who they are and what they're called to so they will get on track and go after His plan fully. When He brings that spouse along, the two callings can merge into a powerful force of the exponential power of two working together to see God's kingdom expanded on the earth.

The truth is: **Understanding your calling is preparation for marriage**.

Consider this: 1+1=2, except in marriage . . . somehow it then equals 1.

Hmmm . . . maybe *our* equation is off.

After all, 1x1 does actually equal 1. God's math is always multiplication, and it's multiplication that happens when we wed. Our combined oneness allows for both WHOLE people to join as one whole unit. The problem is that because marriage is seen as a solution or a fix-all, people rarely consider the need to come into the marriage whole. They often have the perspective that *this will make them whole*. Let's look at that equation again. What happens when we multiply a fraction of a person *(a person who does see themselves as whole)* by another person? We'll never get a whole 1.

$$\tfrac{1}{2} \times 1 = \tfrac{1}{2} \text{ and } \tfrac{1}{2} \times \tfrac{1}{2} = \tfrac{1}{4}!$$

When we come into a marriage broken and feeling incomplete, the marriage simply cannot fix that. In fact, marriage will exacerbate those problems. Suddenly two people who don't feel complete are trying to draw off each other when there's not enough strength for either one! What we're unknowingly asking for is that spouse to be our savior. We're asking another person, not the Lord, to make us whole. It can never work because only One is meant to fulfill that role for us, and He's just waiting for our invitation to do that deeper work within.

Building Your Life

Let me ask a slightly foolish question: *Do you want to be happy?* I don't mean eventually, I'm talking about right now. *Do you desire to feel good about life? Yes?* Good! God wants that for you as well. I hope I'm helping to shatter the perspective that marriage is the goal, because there's a much bigger goal the Lord has in mind, although it will often include (a healthy) marriage. Happiness is something that's for us in every season of life. After all, I highly doubt that the apostle Paul and Jesus were miserable men. But when listening to some folks, that would be the only logical conclusion. In fact, look through the Bible. Isaac must have been plumb unhappy until Rebekah came along when he was 40 years old. The way some people talk, it seems the only way to have joy must surely come from a romantic or sexual relationship. WHERE DID WE GET THIS? Joy was never meant to be supplied to us by people.

There's an old Sunday school song that says,

> *"Don't build your house on a sandy land, don't build it too near the shore.*
> *Well it might look kinda nice, but you'll have to build it twice.*
> *Oh, you'll have to build your house once more.*
> *You gotta build your house on a rock . . ."*

The song is from the story that Jesus tells in Luke 6 of two men who decided to build homes. One man chose to dig down to solid rock and start building. The other decided that he needed the house faster, or maybe it was that the digging took too much work. Whatever the reason, he built on the sand. So, when the storms of life came, the one on the foundation of rock stood strong, but the one on the sand fell hard.

These two men provide a picture for us to understand how to build our own lives. We get to choose the foundation, the building materials, and thereby, much of the outcome rests on us. It's true that our parents or guardians chose a lot for us in the early years, but today we have to acknowledge that we make most choices for our own lives. We can choose to tear down some of what had been built previously or continue to build on it.

I've seen many grow up in godly homes, and although no one's home is "perfect" and many godly homes have more than their share of troubles, good parents try to impart God's truth. However, I've seen those children, as they grow choose to take in hurt and resentment and live life on their own terms—even while still attending church. Eventually, it does catch up, and I've seen many a "good person" embarrassed when the lies they've lived are exposed. You see it's not just what your parents do or don't do—it's what we do with our choices once they are in our hands.

It works both ways though. You may have parents who built on the sand for you. Not teaching the right way to do things, but walking contrary to the things of God. Your choice is if you want to continue to build on that foundation or if you will begin to build on your own, with a new strong foundation.

So how do we "build" our lives? Jesus gives us incredible instruction in that story of the two builders:

> ". . . whoever comes to Me, hears My sayings and does them, I'll tell you who he is like. He is like a man who dug deep and built his house on the rock. When the storms arose and the winds beat vehemently on it, the house would not be shaken because it's foundation was on the rock." (Luke 6:47, 48)

At my home church we refer to this as the *Three Steps to a Solid Life*. It genuinely does apply to every area of our lives. It is how we build our lives on the solid foundation of God's Word and His plan for our lives. First, **come** to Jesus. This isn't just about getting saved, but about making time to go to Him, to seek

Him—daily. This includes attending church, reading our Bible and praying. He always has time for us, but will we take time for Him? Contrary to popular deception, we will never "come" by accident. We will not awake one day with extra time we don't know what to do with and decide to make time for God. Well, at least this approach will never be consistent. We must CHOOSE to come to Him. We must make the time. We must do it on purpose. He is waiting for us to simply "come."

Next, *hear* Him. We have to listen to what He's saying, ask Him to show us and guide us. He wants us to understand. Sometimes we feel like we can't hear God. We don't know what He's saying or how to even listen. Let Him help, He's God. He knows how to get a message to us. Our job is to listen. Jesus made this statement more than once, *"Whoever has ears to hear, let him hear!"* (Mark 4:23) Well, we all have ears, but that's not what He was talking about. He was saying He wants us to listen not only to hear, but also especially to understand and follow. We *are the one He's speaking to*. We must ask the Holy Spirit, who was sent to lead us into Truth (John 16:13), to open our ears. Don't hold back. If you truly want all that God has for you, ask Him right now to come upon you and open your heart to everything He wants for you. Listen. He will speak. He will share His heart with you. It's a privilege we have. God Almighty wants to talk to us. Just take the time to listen to Him.

Finally, He says to *do*. It's simple once we've heard from Him—we just follow through on what we hear. Let me explain that a little. Simple does not mean easy. If it was easy, everyone would be quickly and excitedly following God's plan for their lives, *but they are not*. The reality is that He may ask some pretty tough things of us. He may tell us we need to forgive someone who has wronged us; or maybe He'll ask us to apologize to someone we don't think deserves it. As we ask for wisdom and guidance, *we will get it*. Our job is to pray, thanking Him that He's going to show us what to do, and then trust Him. He knows best. If He says to do something, do it. Our God is so incredible, not only will He tell us what to do to make our life better, but He'll also help us do it if we'll let Him. We just need to "do" what He speaks to us.

Developing a Solid Foundation

The building process doesn't always start with what looks like progress. Have you noticed when a site is chosen for a new building that the first step in "building" is *digging*? As with this story of the builders that Jesus taught, the strength of our life is based on our foundation. You may already know that when talking about a firm foundation, or our solid rock, we immediately look to Jesus. Good. That's true. We can't build anything of substance without Him. Unfortunately, being "Christians" doesn't mean we've got Jesus as our Solid Rock. That should be the case, but it depends on how we build our life. In fact, in this parable, the two builders **both came** to Jesus **and listened** to His words. So, this rock foundation is not only a picture of knowing Jesus, because they both seemed to have that. The difference was that only one of them DUG.

A foundation is drastically different based on the size and height of the intended structure. Additional levels can rarely be added to a completed building because the foundation was never meant to handle that load. People do this with their walk with God. They want the deeper things of God. They want to see God's power flow through them, but they've never dug down to establish their lives solidly upon Him and the absolute certainty of His Word. They simply agree that they love Jesus and move along. There's more to this than even loving Jesus. Our foundation needs work before we can build something significant in our lives. Oftentimes people have never dug at all. Honestly, the digging isn't the fun part. It's not the part where we can see real progress; and many people get frustrated in the digging. We want to have something nice to show off, not to get all dirty and discover the hidden realities of what we're working with.

This is where we have to have the vision in front of us so we don't cast off restraint. Seeing that picture of what God wants to do in and through us is the reality of why we endure the digging process. The realization that when it's done, our Divine Developer has the space and footing to build big and build well! This is why I love having a real, personal God. It is an incredible adventure. He is incapable of planning evil for us. He's crazy about us. We'll discuss that more as we go along, but we need to know that we have a God who is truly and passionately desiring good for us. We have a God who is LOOKING for ways to get the fulfillment and blessing He has for us—*to us*! There's nothing on earth like a life lived truly for Him. The reality is that if God's plan on earth is going to be accomplished through people, then His people need to be able to handle a larger-scale vision than what we've seen in the past. We need to be ready and willing to work with Him to do supernatural things.

This is why digging is important. It's the hard work that establishes the building that He's called us to. When God began to have me dig deeper, I didn't always like what I discovered. Sometimes I uncovered that I was motivated by pride, or that I liked getting attention too much *(and here I thought I was perfect; it's amazing what we find out when we let God show us!)*. If we ask Him, He will show us what debris is down there that would keep us from having a solid foundation. This isn't for the purpose of condemnation or to see how pathetic we are. He is lovingly letting us see the attitudes and issues we've been blindly living with so they can be addressed and cleared out! The freedom and happiness that result from feeling "cleaned out" brings more confidence and expectation in our walk with Him.

In this story, Jesus' picture of that foundation has to do with the one who followed through on step number three: DO. When we listen to Jesus and DO what He says, He will show us where to dig to get all of the old junk out so He can form a beautiful new work in us.

Let me give you a big head start that many Believers miss: You are made up of two very different parts. When you were "born again" your spirit was *born* into God's family, but the rest of you, your thinking and the habits you have, are not re-born. You still need training. You may have noticed that when someone upsets you, you suddenly don't feel so "saved!" Our spirit being born into God's family makes us right with God. However, our mind and emotions need to learn how to "walk right" with God. This is where God has to work with us, and dig things out to help remove the debris that gets in the way of fulfilling His ultimate plan. As we come to Him, hear Him and follow through with our actions, we'll see these are the areas He starts working on first.

I knew a girl named Mary who grew up with a religious background, but she had no personal ongoing relationship with God. When she finally had a real encounter with the Lord, she held nothing back and made a 180-degree turn as fast as she could. She wanted God's ENTIRE plan for her life. She gave up friendships, lifestyles and just about everything else in a passionate sweep to do things God's way. He responded to her choices, rocketing her into a life of ministry and opening up spiritual dynamics in her prayer time that many long-time Believers never touch. She wasn't holding anything back, and God was answering her prayers. The good came along with some tough times. Although she was becoming an encourager to people who had even served God for years longer, her own mind and emotions didn't always keep up with the changes she was making. She was growing like crazy, but was still encumbered by her own thinking and flesh. It was frustrating to her. After all, if she was truly saved, why was she thinking like "that" or acting like "this"? It had nothing to do with how much she was doing right, because although her spirit on the inside was growing, her mind and emotions were fighting to get their way.

The Word says that our flesh (logical mind, emotions and desires) is opposed to what our spirit wants. (Galatians 5:17) In our own lives we see this happen. We want to do right, but we also want to do wrong . . . we're at war on the inside.

In Mary, I watched both the cost and the huge benefits of what happens when a life is given wholly over to God. Her picture for me is beautiful because she didn't just "grow over time" (though we're always still growing), but she went from a party girl to a prayer warrior in the span of what seemed like a few weeks *(though it was a bit longer than that I assure you)*. She did give up many things she liked, and had to change her attitude and check herself on a number of occasions. She even put herself in a very tough situation where she had strong accountability and therefore had to address the ugly side of her emotions or actions when they would show up. When others would just dismiss those issues, she fought for victory over them. From her perspective it would have been easy to think that it wasn't fair for her to *have* to dig so deeply. She could excuse things because the issues she was facing were primarily simply a result of her past; *after all she is only human.* She could have justified her behavior with "well, God knows my heart." But she didn't. The results? I wish you could talk to her. I've seen her stop and declare, "I can't believe the person I was . . . God is so incredible!" You see, she now knows what "life more abundantly" really is. She understands that the Christian life is supposed to be lived as a participator, not a spectator. Only as a participator can we understand the fullness of what God created us to be. Yes, it costs us. In fact, it costs our whole life, but like all good things . . . I should say, all "God things". . . it's well worth it.

For me, some of the deepest digging came when I was asking the Lord about marriage. He began to expose areas in my life that would certainly affect my marriage one day, but I would have never realized . . . until after I got married. Like I mentioned earlier, these directives weren't always my favorite moments.

One of my sisters came to live with me during a season of transition when she was moving into the area. It was great to reconnect with her, but there's something about *family.* You know what I'm talking about don't you? The way a family member can bypass all the really good Christian behavior you feel like you've established and just plain *irritate* you. It's like they have radar to know just where to push to jump over your well-constructed behavior modifications to the *raw gut response.* Yep. That's what she helped me discover . . . my attitudes were not always nearly as holy as I thought they were. There was a particular day, and although I have no recollection of what she said, I clearly remember my response. I just snapped at her. *(I'm sure it was completely and totally justifiable, however.)* Regardless, the Lord spoke to me in that moment and said, "That is how you'll treat your husband." *WHAT? No I wouldn't! I'm going to **love** my husband . . . Oh. Yeah, I love my sister. Hmmm.* That gave me something to chew on. The realization settled in. My husband eventually just becomes my *family.* We will know each other's business and we won't have a lot of fluff that moderates our behavior. It will just be plain gut reaction. So, however my gut reacts, is what he'll get. Apparently, I needed more gut training. To be changed from the inside, not only adjust from the outside . . . that is what digging is all about.

The Lord wants to do a real work in us that is life-long. To address things that will hinder our life, and yes, hinder our marriage. Things like how reliable our word is, which is a big deal to God, and will be to our spouse. What does it take for us to back out of plans we've committed to? Remember, eventually our spouse becomes another person we can beg for their understanding to excuse our bad behavior. The problem is they will be the one we ask the most, and therefore will enjoy those things the least. These are the areas that the Lord will point out, and we will have to determine if we're willing to dig, or if we just want to leave the sand where it is.

It's never too late to go deep, but going deeper takes time. No matter how many years someone walks with the Lord the potential to still need to dig is a reality. Many haven't laid the foundation right because of life circumstances or poor instruction, yet the Lord is the Restorer. He wants us to have the strength of a solid foundation. Digging deeper means we will be stronger and last longer. Deeper means the change is real, not just superficial. Don't get the idea that it happens all at once either. It's easier to *look* deep than to **be** deep. I challenge you to take time to ask the Lord to help you go deeper, to take you to new understanding of your own issues. Ask Him to show you where the old flesh might have control so that He can help you excavate the ground there. If you are willing, He will deepen your foundation to the place where you will not be shaken. If you will seek Him with all your heart, He will be found by you (Jeremiah 29:13–14). You're the one He's waiting on. Are you ready to go deeper?

Prepare Your Home

Proverbs 24:27 says, "*Prepare your outside work, make it fit for yourself in the field; and afterward build your house.*" This verse is the exact opposite of how most (young) singles think. For them, it's, 'I've got to find my mate (get my house together so to speak) and then **together** we'll figure out what "field" the Lord is calling us to.' Scripture takes a different approach. In fact, I believe there's even a piece of the puzzle in this Scriptural approach that many overlook.

First, start by preparing your outside work. There is an honoring of God and stewardship implied in this. The first goal is to make sure we can handle *ourselves.* It's like the Lord is saying, "Don't try to bring someone home into your life until you can sustain a life on your own!" Little did I know that was how the Lord was going to train me.

By the time I was out of college, I was pursing the Lord with gusto. However, I was also looking around every corner to see if maybe my spouse would show up at any minute. I found that the Lord began to prompt me with this scriptural principle, establishing my ministry and employment. I was to be a fully sufficient individual first. So, I did that. I was working fulltime and genuinely trying to keep myself from distractions. I felt like I was on my way toward marriage . . . *any day now. Right Lord?*

Apparently there was another step here, prior to bringing a spouse into the mix. God opened my eyes to this during my annual time of seeking Him for the coming year. I always ask about what areas He's calling me to focus on (these are my "God-given roles."). Each role has a name associated with it. For instance, one role might be "employee," and another, "daughter of God." In 2002, He surprised me with a role I hadn't considered before. As I was prayerfully writing, I heard the word, "homemaker." Please understand; I was single. At the time I rented a room in the home of a family, and trust me, there was no one specific on the horizon. This "homemaker" role seemed like a bit of a far reach. I had neither home nor spouse, so I was a little intrigued as to how the Lord was directing me. As I continued to pray, He began to outline the "areas" in that role I needed to work on. They were things like developing *(and unfortunately maintaining)* a budget, keeping up with my laundry *(so that prior to running out of clothes, I was washing)*, purchasing groceries regularly, even cooking for myself *(instead of take-out? What?).* Now you might suddenly be picturing me as a slob. I assure you it wasn't that bad, but when it came to taking care of me, I was usually last on the list. Therefore my home got the brunt of that as well. He was training me. It was time to learn how to "make a home," even just for myself.

I began to see that "... *build your house"* wasn't only about getting married. It was about knowing how to have a "home." Singles are notorious for either being lazy about taking care of themselves, or being wasteful with money to handle the things they need. Being a homemaker was about not waiting until I married to start dealing with those areas of my life. This is for both guys and gals. It requires a willingness to learn before it becomes an emergency. It's about being responsible and forward thinking in all areas. *Dare I say it?* Growing up.

Ladies and gentlemen, we are all guilty of thinking that "she or he" will be good at "that," because I'm just not. Whatever it is, "that" is an unfair pressure to place on someone. Don't wait to get married to fix your issues! Praise God if they can take up the slack where you struggle, but I'd rather have an incredibly fulfilling marriage with trust and integrity than one where I finally found someone who can take care of the bills! So, are you terrible with finances? Get some help. Grow in that area. Are you someone who leaves everything a mess? Don't think your spouse is going to follow behind you cleaning up after you. Begin to bring order to *your* home. Then the marriage and family can come. Wholeheartedly pursue God's call on your life right now, and make it fit *for yourself* in your job and ministry fields. Then, make your home *fit* too! You'll enjoy living in your space more, and I assure you your spouse will be grateful.

You know that you want to marry someone who has his or her head on straight and wearing clean underwear, so be that kind of person yourself.

Once you are married, you'll have even more things filling up your time and keeping you busy. If you haven't established with clarity ahead of time not only WHAT He's called you to do, but more importantly, that you have a vision of the person He wants you to be, then when will you have time to start on it? Oh, it's absolutely possible to do once you're married, but God has given you this time, right now, to begin that process.

In many cultures, from the time a child is young, even before puberty, they are being specifically trained for marriage. Young girls are taught to cook and sew and many other things. Boys are made to work and take responsibility for labor. From birth they are learning how to be a husband, a wife, a father and a mother. In North American cultures especially, this is more than lacking. It's practically nonexistent. We get to a "marriageable age" and expect to just get married. *That's the preparation?* No wonder we put all our effort into looking for someone to marry. It's the only job we understand is our responsibility.

What if we create a new culture? Not one focused on preparing for marriage so much as **preparing to live whole, God-honoring lives**? We know what our culture has given us: Sky-high divorce rates and unsatisfied people. What if we started doing things differently? Would we see different results?

Along the Way

Through addressing "making it fit for yourself in the field," it's important to focus on a key perspective: As we seek the Lord about how to dig and how to build our life, we will hear instruction and get clarity and vision that will encourage us towards great things (I'm absolutely sure of it!). However, in the midst of pursuing our "calling", we can forget it's not just a job or a position that the Lord is directing us towards. We will have various roles and accomplish certain key tasks that God puts before us, but none of those things are the primary focus of our life. Let me say it this way: Are you called to be a doctor? Great. WHO are you called to be? Are you called to be a Mother? Wonderful, but WHO are you called to be? Maybe you're going to be a plumber. I'm glad, but WHO are you called to be? You see, it's WHO we are called to be, not WHAT we are called to do that makes the difference to God.

This is why coming to Him, hearing Him and obeying is so important. We're setting a life pattern for the kind of person we are and will become. More importantly, we'll be setting a pattern that our family will follow to be people who pursue God's will above our own. There are so many verses that escape our understanding of the Lord as our strength and our protector, but many of them come with a certain assumption or caveat that we're dwelling or abiding IN Him. Again, we've had this "Christian paradigm" that once I call Jesus "Lord" the rest is up to God. We haven't considered how we truly "abide" or "dwell" in the Lord. Contemplate these:

- *"He who dwells in the secret place of the most high, shall abide in the shadow of the Almighty . . ." (Psalm 91:1)*
- *"I am the vine, you are the branches. He who abides in Me, and I in him, bears much fruit; for without Me you can do nothing." (John 15:5)*

I think it's stated most clearly from God's perspective in Psalm 91:9–11, *"Because you have made the Lord . . . your dwelling place, no evil shall befall you, nor shall any plague come near your dwelling for He shall give His angels charge over you . . ."* We overlook poetic verses at times when the Holy Spirit just as much inspired those as the gospels. Here in this Psalm, God responds with a declaration of why protection is extended over this person; and it has to do with how they "abide" in God. Abiding is living. Living in God is not a complicated matter, but it's certainly not something we should suppose occurs because we go to church or we say we love God. I can say I love my parents, but the fact is that they live thousands of miles from me and I don't have an everyday understanding of their desires or plans. I don't "abide" with them and certainly not in them. To abide in the Lord is what He addresses in John 15: That we recognize our utter dependency on Him and that He is our source. He's the vine, or the trunk of the tree, as it were. Our own sustenance relies upon what He gives. For those of us in a culture or home that has food on the table each day and clothes on our backs (whether we like them or not), we don't really understand what this kind of dependency looks like. So when God asks for that, we think we yield to Him, when in fact we just acknowledge Him and go about our way.

To abide in the Lord is to come to a new understanding of what it means to be without Him. To abide in the Lord is to set our mind each day on Him and His desires. This is not mealtime prayers from memory and rote bedtime prayers. It's the living breathing relationship of two beings interacting and interconnecting, with us wholly aware of our dependency on Him. Moses said it best when God told Him that He'd send an angel with them into the land, because He (God) was no longer going to come. Moses response was, *"If your Presence does not go with us, do not bring us up from here . . ."* (Exodus 33:15) This simple reality declares that I do not want to go anywhere He is not. I do not want to pursue anything He is not a part of. I only want to abide in Him.

This is what He wanted me to understand as I began to "prepare" for marriage and "prepare" my life. I was supposed to be "becoming" the woman He'd called me to be, not just the spouse or person that someone else would one day appreciate.

That's what He wants you to understand. You are precious to Him and He does have good things in store for you. It's not His will that you have to figure things out alone. Just because you don't feel like you can hear Him, doesn't mean you can't. He's well able to get a message through to you, but you must commit in your heart that you will follow Him.

SECTION THREE

The Reality of Relationships

I know by this point you may be thinking, 'Finally! I thought she was just going to tell me to wait on God and my spouse would magically appear!'

Actually, I'm not going to tell you how to find a spouse at all. I'm not even going to tell you TO find a spouse. This was not written to dictate structures or styles of approach to relationships. I've heard debates about *courting* versus *dating* and such, and there are valid points to be addressed. The issue simply isn't the label associated with what we do. With God, the issue is ALWAYS the heart. So I want to address more of "how" we approach relationships and not the style of approach or what to call it. I don't know about you, but I just want to know what God says about something. Once I understand that, I can walk out my part of that equation with confidence. Too often a lot of "godly people" give their opinion, and although their intention is appreciated, we need to understand God's perspective more.

My goal is to share Scripture with you, along with biblical perspective. Within that I will also share personal insights and my perception, especially as it relates to our present-day culture. As you read these next pages, you will need to stop and ask the Lord for yourself, "How should I approach this area?" The more time we spend with Him and getting to know His Word, the easier it is to align our life to His purpose for us. Being led astray will get more and more difficult because on the inside of us it just doesn't align with what we know about Him. Of course, there are PLENTY of people who would like to give their opinions . . . and more often than not it has a lot less to do with what Scripture says and more to do with how it worked (or didn't work) for them *(not that I'm speaking from experience of my own married friends who would NEVER try to direct me with their own experience as the guide)*. Truthfully, sometimes our flesh will really want to agree with what they say, usually because it seems like that might work faster or better. Remember what we're choosing: We will live a God-honoring life that puts all our faith in Him *and not in ourselves*. It's these well-meaning people that often allow deception to creep into the church because we go with what we *feel* and *think* instead of finding out what God actually *says*.

Consider the concept of dating I presented earlier. Dating is something that was developed by secular society. The way we approach this area in the church differs some, but all in all, it's based on a secular approach to relationships. It's a funny thing to me because I simply cannot think of one time in the Bible where we see God instruct His people to follow the routes, customs or behaviors of the other nations. *Oh, but wait, we do have certain "boundaries" in Christian dating.* All right, yet I cannot find a single time in all of Scripture where God instructed his people to do what the nations around them were doing, but to instead create some adjusted boundaries for it. *Really? Where did we get this?*

One of the big problems we face today is that society and its approaches have crept into the church in many areas. It seems "silly" to think we'd handle relationships drastically differently. After all, it's become more common to have premarital sex. So things are changing . . . right?

Well, it is true that things have changed, but how much we permit that change to affect our lives demands that we understand God's Word. It's not that everything that is acceptable in our culture is by nature truly evil, but that we have to have some way to test it. It's not by our rationale or logic either. The ONLY way to judge something is not by what's "acceptable" to people, but by weighing it against Scripture to see what's acceptable to God.

When my parents were growing up, people dated someone different every week. They constantly "dated." They spoke about these relationships like they were a lot of good, clean, fun. I grew up thinking that's how I would be. I would just date lots of guys and we'd hang out and have fun. However, by the time I was in high school, things had changed quite a bit. First, dating was an exclusive practice. You didn't date someone else, until you had "broken up" with the previous person. This culture shifted as I got older, but it still holds somewhat true in most high schools. So, dating lots of guys would mean developing and terminating multiple committed relationships. That seemed like less fun than what mom and dad talked about.

In fact, for me, things were even stranger. I chose not to date in high school, much to the consternation of my parents, let me assure you! Most parents would love to have their teenager more interested in their future than dating. However, my parents felt like a healthy balance of both was in order . . . so they didn't quite know what to make of me. Now, honestly, they weren't the only ones who thought it was odd *(not that I really announced that I wasn't dating; in fact it wasn't so much an absolute choice, but I just opted out when asked)*. Making that choice certainly didn't stop my mind or heart from behaving like a typical teenager *(I reread some old journals and couldn't believe the words I had written, I really thought I was way more spiritual than all of that! Ha!)*. I didn't know how long this "not dating" thing would last, but I was convinced that the Lord had only what was best for me in mind. He'd rescued me out of such an ugly place in life. Now that I had joy, I wasn't about to trade it in to start doing things my way.

In fact, He began to show me how to "renew my mind" about relationships in that season of my life. I really started seeing things differently. It was like I suddenly looked around and realized there was very little chance that I was going to marry any of these guys. Not because they were bad guys *(I did go to a Christian school, so I could have easily presumed that the chances were higher that I would marry one of them)*, but because I had started catching a glimpse of the life God had for me. I felt inside of me that I was going to "go" and "do" something. I had no idea what, but it didn't seem to include settling down quite yet. For many, realizing they aren't going to marry their boyfriend or girlfriend has nothing to do with continuing to date them. I had felt the same way, but that's when the Lord sort of hit me with another reality: *If I'm not going to marry him, why would I invest my time, energy or emotion and give (even in small ways) of myself physically?* In the end, one or both of us would be hurt. It's inevitable. I suddenly saw dating as toying with someone's emotions . . . or my own. It just didn't seem fair to either of us. Little did I realize God was beginning to form my thoughts in this area, and set me up to be protected from a lot of future dangers.

As high school ended, I set the idea of "dating" aside. I went to college with no intention of avoiding dating, but with a real understanding that I didn't want to date for the sake of dating. I loved having guys and girls around as friends, but I just wasn't going to give my heart away too quickly. I was beginning to understand that God was calling me *not* to trust in me, but *to* trust in Him. Did I believe He could arrange this area of my life? Did I doubt His love and goodness? Did I realize He had someone great in store? Would I let Him take the lead on that?

Thus, I never made a choice to "not date," I just didn't. I chose to ask God to help me define the boundaries I needed and to become the person I was meant to be. From then, He began to do even more work in me.

It's funny, because movies in the past decade or so have come out that talk about being a virgin or never having been kissed and the only possible movie reality to these options is that the person is just so very homely and even uncouth that they couldn't get a date to save their lives.

First of all, that's not even possible anymore. There's enough nastiness out there that if a person just wants some physical satisfaction, they can get it. It's really not a challenge. What is a challenge is staying pure. What is a challenge is being emotionally and spiritually healthy. What is a real challenge is not allowing ourselves to be led by culture's expectations and influence to do or become something other than what God designed us for. THAT is challenging. I made the choice. I'm up for the challenge.

Healthy Boundaries

If you're single, you've experienced this: The times where life pushes you around, knocks you down and you feel it—Loneliness. We just wish there was *someone* there. It may be as innocent as just wanting someone to cuddle with in front of the TV, but instead it's just you *and the TV*. Not a terribly comforting evening ahead. Whether male or female, you've likely had that one draining day that you made the mistake of ending with a movie *(maybe a romance or even a totally unromantic movie that had a romance sub-plot or an unromantic movie that you could imagine a romantic edge to . . . gee, it could just be a sci-fi robotic relationship),* and you walked away from the theater or turned off the TV to sigh and think, 'When is that coming for me?' Or it may actually have been after visiting family or friends with small children and seeing that family dynamic and realizing you aren't even close to that yet, and thought the same, or better yet, 'OK Lord, I'm ready anytime now . . .' *(again, we're SO GOOD at reminding the Lord about things He must be missing).* It's those days, and nights, that can be a killer for singles . . . yet somehow we need to be strong.

When I say to be strong, I'm not talking about simple tenacity and discipline, although it will definitely take some of that. What I'm talking about is different. It's being steadfast and immovable, because of our trust and faith in God. Once we're convinced that God WILL do what He said, we aren't as concerned about WHEN He's going to get around to it. Instead we are confident. That's the strength we need to see us through. It's a strength that is at rest in God's promises.

Picture this: You are getting into a brand new Porsche Cayenne for a test drive. You have zero thoughts that this vehicle might break down. You are at rest. However, when you get back into your 1983 Datsun 280ZX with a hole rusted in the floor and windshield wipers that actually don't stop running *(do I sound like I'm speaking from experience here?),* your faith can tend to be a little less impressive. The point is that if we believe something we act on it, and our behavior changes based on our faith. When we're convinced of something, we rest in that knowledge. When we're unsure of something, we wonder, or fret or fear, or question and create alternate plans.

If we believe that we may not receive the promises God has for us, then we will behave that way, searching and worrying about how to make things happen for ourselves. I don't want to live like that. I cannot live like that; partially because I realize I have too many important things to accomplish! *I don't even know what they all are*, but I do know that God has a plan for my life! Worry will hinder that. If we waste our time trying to figure out how to accomplish what He's already planning to provide for us, then although we will be busy, it will be a complete waste of time. Besides, what we can do on our own will never be as good as if we had let Him do it His way!

How do we get to that place of rest? It's a pretty simple path, but it's certainly one that needs to be sought after. Romans 10:17 says, *"Faith comes by hearing and hearing by the word of God."* Just hearing the exhortations of this book are helping build faith. Get some Scriptures and HEAR them. Speak them out loud, memorize them and meditate on them. Convince yourself of what God says instead of what everyone is telling you. This faith will give you the undergirding you need to fulfill your calling, to operate beyond yourself, and to wait for God's perfect timing for marriage! As we are being changed and learning to approach life in a new way, we need to have some practical boundaries and guidelines to help us keep from naïvely, or sometimes intentionally, making poor choices. Thoughts come. Feelings come. Situations present themselves and give us opportunities to satisfy our flesh. Or we can decide to submit to His Spirit. But how can we make sure that we will make the right choice? **"In the moment" is a bad time to start considering the options.** In fact, the more we succumb to temptations, the stronger the hold they have on us. As one who has not succumbed very much, I can tell you the thoughts and desires still come. This is where two big decisions have made the difference for me:

1) When I submit myself to God and purpose to walk pure before Him, He has permission to step in at a different level. When He's *really* the "Lord" of my life, when danger comes, He'll help me sound the alarm. If I listen, I'll be sure to hear it next time. He is a rescuing God and I can

attest to the fact that there were times when my flesh would have made the wrong decision, but He stepped in and the circumstance was practically taken away from me. THANK YOU LORD!

2) Having clear guidelines and boundaries that I hold to no matter what makes a huge difference. If I know "I never . . ." or "I always . . .", then when unhealthy opportunities present themselves, I'll already be in a safe place. I don't have to wait and see.

When we don't have clarity on what's OK and what's not, but our decisions are conditional, we will be in a dangerous place for Satan's snares. He's the master of 'little by little'. He will woo a person into complacency and make a sneak attack when they thought they were safe. What are we so afraid of missing out on? The truth is that there are (rare) times when some physical contact can be innocent. The problem is what seems innocent on the outside may not be on the inside of one of the people. When that happens, who is going to say, "Wait! I'm struggling with this. We should stop."? No one likes to sound weak, and more so we usually convince ourselves "just a little" will be okay. Those occasions that begin innocently can even become dangerous. When our mind is less alert, like when we're tired (also a danger in hanging out late) or during seasons when we've felt lonely . . . these kinds of interactions can be just what's needed to tilt us downhill. Some of us can attest to how quickly something "innocent" becomes something . . . um, well . . . NOT innocent. I once had a lady tell me when discussing the difficulty of staying pure, "Never let a guy rub your ear." I wanted to laugh as it seemed like such a funny warning, but soon enough I discovered, it was a very true one. The fact is that what seems like the most "harmless" thing, can lead us someplace we don't want to be.

Emotional boundaries are just as important as physical ones if we really want to live this life in a way that's honoring to the Lord and to the people we interact with. It's our decisions up front that will help establish our character and help us remain steady when situations are primed to pull us down.

Friendships (Emotional Boundaries)

My grandparents were from Czechoslovakia. Since English wasn't their first language, some words never quite made the translation. Granny used to talk about how "big" my sister's hair was (she meant "long") and asked if we had any "friend-boys" (of course meaning "boyfriends"). I would tell her, "Yes Granny, I have *lots* of friend-boys!" Of course, that would get quite a wide-eyed response from her *(come to think of it, I never told her what I really meant, I may have some repenting to do in heaven . . . if that's possible)*. My sister and I liked the word, and we began to use it as a way to signify when a guy was really "just a friend". He was a "friend-boy."

Now, I have always been close to my father, and therefore my personality was, in some ways, a little more tomboyish. Not obviously so, but I just always enjoyed hanging out with "the guys." In fact, I preferred it. Yet, I'm not a guy, and my friendships with guys often created interesting dynamics that I wasn't always aware of. When a guy offered me a ride home or thought we should grab a coffee *(I know, I sound terribly naïve! I'm sorry, I just didn't see myself that way, so I didn't think they would!)* I thought, 'Sure! Great! Love hanging out with new friends!' For some reason I was oblivious to the fact that they were thinking a little more *boyfriend* than *friend-boy*. The strange thing was, although I was the one turning them down *(I'm not talking about hundreds of men, these were mostly high school situations, and I was an unattached girl who hung out with them; it wasn't like I was prom queen)*, somehow I ended up getting hurt. Repeatedly. I began to not trust men at all; I felt betrayed, or at least lied to. They said we were friends, but then when I didn't want to date them, they disappeared. Was my only value in being a girlfriend? I started getting a bit leery of having friend-boys at all.

This is a difficult topic to address because to this day, I connect well with men and find them easier (at times) to have a casual acquaintance with. I'm not a super-emotional girl and I like the laidback approach to friendship that guys more often function in. However, I've drastically adjusted my approach to friendships with males. Most young adults will tell you it's absolutely possible to have platonic male-female friendships. This can be true when they stay very distant, but from what I've both seen and experienced personally, a genuine friendship will get very messy and complicated before it has the strength (if the people stick it out) to return to a genuinely platonic one.

Because of this, I've intentionally stopped pursuing friendships with men. Not in the "run for your life" way, but when guys show up whom I can see I'd get along with, my first step is to pray. Yes, that's right. I pray. I pray for a few reasons. It's not just a *"Lord, is he the one?"* prayer. It's actually more of a *"Should I allow this friendship?"* prayer. That may seem pretty strange to some. For me it's a respect issue; respecting the Lord and respecting these guys. I've seen the look on my male *friends'* faces when we realize we've been under two different expectations about the friendship. Or the feeling in my gut when I realize that guy *I didn't think I was interested in* started dating that other girl. The fact is, I don't want to injure anyone, and I certainly don't want to allow my own heart to be broken when it isn't necessary. So before my emotions start to cloud my judgment, I pray.

God brings good friends, and there have been times when I felt like He prompted me to reach out to a guy in some way. Those are not the common times though. Usually, I feel like He will caution me and keep me at a distance. For many years, it was more about guarding my own heart. So, though my heart stayed pretty secure, I unintentionally hurt others. Then came the times when I thought I was guarding my own heart, but allowing too much time together, which naturally led to confusing emotions. It's taken years for me to realize, but I have to choose that I will not interfere with someone else's calling. I certainly don't want others to mess with mine. Yes, I did say "calling". You may not think about it that way, but that's what relationships have the potential to do. Our spouse will either release us to be all we're called to be, or potentially hinder our walk with the Lord and even our ultimate calling in life and ministry. It's not about being bad or good; it's simply the way people are wired. I've become very dependent on the Lord for wisdom in this area of my life. I realize I can't figure it out all on my own. The truth is, now I'm more prone to keep a distance and cautiously allow more time because I know that the Lord doesn't want me to miss something good He has for me. However, my flesh still wants . . . well, what it wants. I'd rather have to be prompted by the Lord than corrected.

There's a reality that I denied for years because I don't tend to function in a stereotypically female fashion, but I've finally come to accept: Guys and girls really do think differently. It's just true. We were created to think differently—to compliment one another. That means that even the way we look at friendship is different. Initially, when boy meets girl, or at least they start to get to know one another, the question is asked internally: Could this be "the one?" *(Or for some, "Could this be another one?").* From my experience, once a girl answers this question, it is answered. In other words, a gal will meet a guy and think, 'Hmm, could anything ever happen here?' Once she has decided, 'No,' it's done. Unless something major transpires, or they end up with a very long-term friendship, that answer simply stands. On the other hand, guys don't make a once-and-for-all decision. They will tend to think, 'No, I don't think so.' However, next weekend she may smile just the right way, or they may have a good conversation, or she may even just wear a great outfit and he's thinking, 'You know, I really like her a lot.' Suddenly the door is open again. This is where I got hurt those many years ago. When a guy agreed that we were "friends", he was not saying we'd never be something else, but that it was good to be friends for now. Some of them were already intent on the next step. For me, that was a violation of what was said. Friend just means friend.

This is especially important because I feel like I've heard so many people say, "We talked about it and we're just going to be friends." **Ladies**, let me say that really doesn't settle <u>anything</u>. To a guy, that's still an open door. **Guys**, I will say to you: She's NOT leaving an open door when she says "friends." She's talking about you being an "uncle" to her babies one day.

Not only in the area of friendship do we think differently. It's well known that guys tend to be physically stimulated whereas women tend to be more emotionally stimulated. For some males, a girl simply giving him a hug can send all kinds of improper thoughts through his head. For a girl, just one time that he's there with a strong shoulder to cry on can make him a strength in her life, even in place of God. This girl or this guy may have every good intentions and pure motives, but the fact is that these friendships are difficult to keep from causing complications and danger.

You many think this is overstated, but I would challenge you to talk to a married couple you look up to and find out how many opposite-sex friends they each have. Not friends who are couples, but people they would individually call on as a friend; someone who is not his or her same gender. The truth is, once we marry, the lines get a whole lot clearer—*and our spouse helps with that*. It's not about not trusting. It's about the fact that we were meant to "leave and cleave" and when we get a guy and a girl together for long, especially alone, something somewhere will start to stir. Call it biology, call it preconditioning to procreate, but it's true.

It was when I was in the midst of a "friend-boy" relationship going screwy that I finally started understating this at a deep level. I knew people who said, "You shouldn't have guy-girl friendships. They never work," yet I was so predisposed to hanging out with guys that I rejected that as silly. I'm not sure I completely agree with it now, but I'll say this: I would never recommend guy-girl friendships, and I know I would caution against them.

I started hanging out with this guy on and off and usually with a few others. He was cool, loved God and was really in the middle of getting his life back together. He was a little older than me and my mind started doing the whole *"Maybe it's him?"* game. We started spending a lot of time together. It was weird because initially it was so platonic that it seemed like there was no danger at all. I didn't see any warning signs. It wasn't until I realized I didn't want to admit to how much time we spent together, how often we texted each other, and how often we were on the phone that I saw how NOT platonic it looked *from the outside*. I was quite convinced I was still guarding my heart. I was pretty sure he wasn't really interested in me anyway. But sometimes we'd hang out until so late that as he was dropping me off at my apartment, I was thinking, 'What if he kissed me right now? Would I stop him?' *In case you're confused, those are not platonic thoughts.*

The Lord gave me a verse that drove the reality home.

"A prudent man foresees evil and hides himself; the simple pass on and are punished." (Proverbs 27:12)

It is important to hide yourself from the evil you see, but also that which you can "*fore*see." The wisest man who ever lived, Solomon, is telling us by the inspiration of the Holy Spirit, to "look ahead" and to "consider what could be coming" and then hide ourselves from the evil or dangerous possibilities. I got the funniest picture in my mind of hiding behind a big rock while the path around me seemed clear and safe, with only a hint of a dust cloud on the other side of the hill down that path. That idea of being willing to look silly, hiding myself from what could be damaging, while everyone else thinks it's all-safe, is a good mental image and reminder to be prudent.

One of my initial encounters that got a little physical should have been enough to warn me away from that friend of mine. Oh, it seemed innocent at first. He was just showing someone else how to demonstrate affection toward your girlfriend in little ways. I was the test subject. It really wasn't anything overly sexual, but the reality was that it was more than what's appropriate between friends. I let the warning signs go by. Why? Probably because I liked it. Afterward, I felt dumb. I knew I shouldn't have permitted that, but there were others around who validated that it was no big deal, so I let their judgment guide me. I behaved as what Proverbs calls "simple." I will tell you, after one of the weirdest and most distracting seasons of my life, in accordance with Scripture, I was corrected. I can say it wasn't nearly what it could have been, but I'm so grateful for the chastisement of the Lord that finally pulled me off that path. It was dangerous and I was playing with fire.

Can I speak directly to you from my experience and years of hearing testimony after testimony? Do not be fooled. You may not think it's a big deal, but the punishment for not paying attention is not worth it. It's not the friendships in general that are the problem, it's how close we allow them to get. Only one person of the opposite gender was made to be our best friend and that's our spouse. WARNING: If you feel like you are drawn to someone of the opposite sex and enjoy his or her company and conversation more than anyone else, but you don't feel like God is giving you the green light for a future marriage relationship—*step back*. It may be very hard, but this is what may save both of you from grief, heartbreak, compromise and punishment in the end. Trust me, if you're willing to FOREsee potential danger, you are much less likely to encounter dangerous situations. You will have more peace and less confusion and you will do the same for your friend-boy or friend-girl. To top it off, your devotion to your future spouse will grow stronger. When you're married, the opportunities to draw near to someone else of the opposite sex will sound warning bells much more quickly if you've been training yourself that way for years.

By the way, even with friends, it's important to have boundaries. Things like being intentional to hang out in groups if you're not dating. The group will definitely make note if you start acting like you are dating when you've said you're not. It's built-in accountability. Phone calls should be brief. You do not need to share deeply with someone of the opposite sex that is not your future mate. Now if one call is long, it's not evil, but if you have long calls each day or each week, you are building emotional ties you will eventually have to break. Text messaging should not be a daily thing . . . it's sowing into those emotional ties. Be willing to open up to an accountability partner even about a "friend." Let them ask you about your thoughts and feelings. Be open. This is you foreseeing possible danger and keeping yourself from it.

Pursuing Relationships (Emotional Boundaries)

I shared about a personal valley I walked through with a male friend of mine. Now I call that season of my life the time when I was "fake-dating." I had prayed. I knew I had no "green light" about that guy as a potential husband. I was just not willing to walk away. I kept hoping he'd become "the one." I can also honestly say at this point that my prayers weren't too fervent once I felt like I wasn't getting more of a sense of "caution" from the Lord either. They sort of dwindled off. I continued to spend time with him, grew close, but did everything I could to still make things seem right. All in all, it was completely unhealthy *(I wish I could have seen what I was doing from a different angle; I would have smacked myself upside the head)*.

Just so we're clear: That's not the picture of "not dating" I was talking about. That's a picture of "dumb." There are two ways we could approach starting a relationship:

1) A Word From God

A great guy I know approached me recently with a gleam in his eyes. He was excited to share with me the story of how the Lord pointed out his future bride to him and he was excited to become her husband. I was happy for him. Then he informed me that I was that woman! I was surprised, but apparently not as surprised as he was that I wasn't already onboard. He was sure he'd heard from God. He's a sane, healthy Christian man whom I respect. I didn't think he was smokin' something, but I knew I wasn't on the same page. I told him I'd pray about it (to respect his spiritual sense), but I simply didn't get peace in that direction from the Lord. So I graciously declined his offer . . . *to date or get married or whatever it was.*

Let's address this in more detail. In Charismatic Christian circles the concept of hearing from God is much more prevalent, and therefore can become a dangerous way that we "take the Lord's name in vain." Our emotions can speak very loudly and we can misinterpret our senses. When we attach God's name to those things, we're certainly misrepresenting Him. This is one area I feel He gets constantly blamed. I've heard more people say, "God told me I'm going to marry so-and-so," than I've seen marry so-and-so. This can be a very hurtful and awkward situation for both people. I want to give some very practical guidelines for walking down this kind of path.

First, it's absolutely possible for God to tell you who your future spouse is. I warn you that if you're hearing this "out of season" (in other words, you're in high school, or in a situation where it's not time to be married, or you're taking time off from relationships to focus on God), then you have a pretty safe bet that either Satan is enticing you or your "heart" is in the lead on this one. It's not absolute, but you need to set it aside and let the Lord lead you when that season changes.

Second, if you do hear this from the Lord, HE is also responsible to tell your future spouse. That isn't your role. Now, inviting them out to coffee or dinner, getting to know them a little bit, and at an appropriate juncture sharing that you have been praying about this and you are very excited to continue getting to know them is good. One reason to approach it this way is so that if they do not feel that way, there's an open door for them to address it. You DO NOT want to pressure someone to marry you. You may not look at it like that, but if this person has to disagree about whether you heard from the Lord, then they feel that they either: 1) Are not hearing God; 2) Will seem mean or insensitive; or 3) Choose to trust your sense, and after you're engaged or married they may be really confused about whether they made the right choice. **Both people need to be clear on what they're hearing for themselves.**

Third, "knowing" doesn't equate to getting married quickly. Now, depending on various factors, such as your spiritual and physical maturity, a quick marriage isn't a bad thing; but it's just not a given either. Once you start down certain roads, it's hard to slow down. At the same time, marriage is forever and you want to make sure you're approaching it with the wherewithal to make sure God is in the center of your decisions.

2) A General Sense of Peace

What should it look like if I don't have a Word from God? Well, that's probably where most people will find themselves, and it will look different for each situation. Some will feel like they "know" the moment they meet. For others, it will be after some time of getting to know a person that led to that place of "knowing." For others still, they might spend a lot of time around each other serving in ministry and after one "date" feel like they're convinced.

It doesn't need to follow a certain pattern, but here's what's critical:

1) You're completely trusting in the Lord for his direction.
2) You pray BEFORE your emotions get too involved. PLEASE HEAR THIS: Emotions mess with us. I mentioned in the

preface what the Book of Joel warns us about. Our hearts deceive. If you're not already seeking God before that first date, it may be too late to get a clear sense.

3) You keep praying and allowing the Lord to caution, correct or encourage you. Remember that until you're married, you're only accountable to the Lord and whatever authority He's placed over you. Your (possible) intended is not the one to dictate how quickly you will both move.

4) Be accountable. Find someone (of the same gender as you) who understands you're strong convictions or who is even stronger in these areas than you, and talk about what you're doing in detail. What your sense of things has been, etc.

If you can keep these four guidelines in the forefront of your thinking, you will be honoring the Lord and keeping your heart (as well as his or hers) from the snares that Satan would like to set for you.

How Far Is Too Far? (Physical Boundaries)

We addressed the issue of Lordship already. You belong to the Lord. When it comes to dealing with physical boundaries in relationships, for too long we've been asking the wrong questions. The question should not be "How much can I get away with?" or even "How far can we go?" but "What honors the Lord?"

Seriously, I've heard way too many Christians talk about every area of their lives as though their goal is to "not sin" instead of to "live God's abundant life." We're asking the wrong questions! We've entered into a covenant with the Lord. We told Him we're committed to Him above all else. *But it's a lie. We lie, to ourselves first, and ultimately to Him and others*. We come to church and act as though He's our priority and then we walk out those doors and fill our list of priorities with so many other things. We treat God like He's just the first check to mark off on the list instead of a part of everything on our list. We treat Him like we can check off "God" after we attend church and then get on with the rest of our lives. *He IS our life*. At least, He's supposed to be.

Imagine getting married to someone and instead of desiring to make him or her happy, to put a smile on their face, our only goal is to not "tick him or her off." That's it. We feel good so long as we didn't cross a line into what's displeasing. Everything else doesn't matter. We fulfill the lowest possible denominator. How do we think our spouse would respond to that relationship? Well, probably in like kind. Neither of us would enjoy our marriage.

So why do we treat God that way? Do we think He doesn't actually care about our lives? That as long as we don't cross the big bad official *sin line*, then everything else is no big deal? Instead we think, *'It's all good. God knows my heart.'* Blah, blah, blah. Honestly? Try that with your friends for a while and see how it goes.

This is why, when dealing with physical boundaries, we have to go to Scripture; not just for the "sin" line, but to see how God talks to us about these areas. There are two very clear biblical mandates:

> *"The wife does not have authority over her own body but the husband does. And likewise the husband does not have authority over his own body, but the wife does."* *(1 Corinthians 7:4)*

#1 Once we're married our body belongs to our spouse.

> *"Or do you not know that your body is a temple of the Holy Spirit who is in you, whom you have from God, and you are not your own?" (1 Corinthians 6:19)*

#2 Our body doesn't belong to us . . . it's not ours to give.

Oh, I know that right now you may be raising an eyebrow and thinking, *'You mean, we can't do . . . anything?'* I didn't say that *(then again, I also didn't <u>not</u> say it)*. I'm hoping you can see this a little more clearly as we dissect a better understanding of abstinence.

Let's address that one **big** sin line that seems to become more and more confused as time goes by. There's a big fat lie floating around that everyone has sex and that it's normal. You're weird if you don't. Yes, it's true that premarital sex is now normal in this day and age, yet years ago it was unacceptable even in our secular society. Of course even though by far, not "everyone" is sleeping around in junior high and high school, perception is more important than reality. Sometimes it's just excluding certain truths that allow everyone to believe what he or she thinks is true. If those partial truths make someone seem more cool, then they will continue to permit them to float around.

The truth is, most people don't get over the high school "looking cool" phase. People want to be perceived as cool, so we talk like we know more than we do. We act like things are *so obvious;* yet we've really got no idea about them. If we'll look weird to others if they knew we weren't sexually active, then we'll just not mention that.

We certainly don't need to announce it to everyone, but it's amazing to me how this pressure to seem like we're just like everyone else can control us. At this point in my life, I'm probably on the furthest edge of not caring what people think when it comes to these things. In fact, I was at a friend's birthday celebration a few years back and met a mutual friend who was a bartender. We started chatting and he quickly made a comment (in a positive way) about how I wasn't "like most girls." He'd grown up in a very strict sect of a religious group and he knew I was very committed to my relationship with God, though he admittedly walked away from anything to do with Him. It was like he suddenly had a realization as he spoke to me and asked, "Wait, are you still a virgin?" Now, to the average person that would have been awkward . . . shoot, a few years prior it would have been awkward for me. But God grows us, and in that moment, I just laughed. I answered affirmatively and he began to reel with such a confused look on his face. It was like he couldn't comprehend that someone who was normal and 'chill' could not be sexually active. I apparently didn't seem to be "the type." It just reaffirmed the fact that people don't really know. If we hadn't gotten as deeply as we did into our conversation, he wouldn't have guessed. In fact, he would have just assumed the opposite. The icing on the cake for me was that as he told me how he didn't know anyone over 25 who was still a virgin, I noted to myself that at least five people at the party whom I knew were, including our mutual friend! He simply had no idea.

The unarguable truth is that sex was only ever intended for marriage. All sexual acts are meant for *that* bed alone. There are so many ways people are now being sexually satisfied that we've made exceptions for. It's all right to do such-and-such as long as you don't have intercourse. This came from that same line of thinking that says, "*What can I get away with?*" That's not living in a "How do I honor God?" perspective. It's a "How do I satisfy my flesh?" perspective that WILL lead to destruction.

This is also why marriage doesn't cure lust. Please hear me: MARRIAGE DOES NOT CURE LUST. Lust is never satisfied. I've seen the horrible damage caused in marriage when one partner was so bound before marrying, but thought this holy union would fix the issue. No, it's never satisfied and your spouse is not the one meant to heal you, Jesus is. If you have bondage to lust, you absolutely must address it before you enter into marriage. Your spouse will be damaged by your behavior and the one you swore to honor is the one you will hurt. Whether its pornography, self pleasure, or any other form of bondage, these things will only cause more grief the longer they are permitted. You are not alone in these bondages and God is well able to heal you. Call out to Him. Get yourself into the Word of God and get rid of those things that give you access to that behavior. Your life is at stake.

Let me give you something else to seriously consider: First Corinthians 7:5 talks about married people "depriving" one another for a time. Most married couples somehow forget that this is in their Bible *(I've brought it up before and it always causes quite the laughter like, "God surely didn't mean that!")*. But there's a powerful reality to it. Paul is talking about fasting sexual relations as a married couple to instead focus on the Lord. As I read that a few years ago I was again reminded how powerful our relationships are. How we can come to depend on each other and not the Lord. I was also reminded that marriage doesn't heal lust and fasting is a good way to ensure both parties are keeping their focus where it needs to be.

Being abstinent as a single person is not a punishment or a "cross to bear," it's actually honoring. It honors God first as the One we trust and seek to please. It honors our own body, keeping ourselves from being wrapped up in bondages that God never wanted to drag us down. Ultimately, it honors our spouse. We have made a choice that we value him or her so much we never want any form of sexual act to take us to another place or another person. We will always be only theirs.

If you've crossed and crisscrossed and re-crossed these boundaries already, please do not be disheartened. God has restored some of the most "pure" people I know from a very impure past. You are not disqualified. The decision you have to make though is the same one that a virgin needs to make: I WILL wait. You have a chance to have God restore your virginity, spiritually speaking. To cleanse away the past and make you new. You may have even been married, but the Lord sees where you are today. If you're willing to give Him all of you He will do a wonderful work in your life. I've seen it multiple times, and you're no exception.

Whether for the first time or the only time, holding this line will be tough. However, I can assure you that it's easier the less physical contact you have. It may seem pretty obvious, but two fully clothed people in a public place are less likely to do something they shouldn't than when you get "alone" with someone of the opposite sex. I've known at least four couples in the last two years who shared their fist kiss at the altar. Like guessing someone is a virgin, you wouldn't look at any of these couples and think they were super-stuffy or rigid and religious. It was amazing to find this out because none of them were under some "rule" or new teaching that came through their churches to wait for their first kiss. In fact, I don't know if any of them actually had their very first kiss ever at the altar, but it was the first they shared with each other. I know one couple that had been more physically affectionate who decided to cut that off when they got engaged! Their determination to stay pure was so strong that they said they didn't want to have any regrets when they got married, so they kept to holding hands through that entire season! I didn't influence any of them in these decisions, but what I do know is that each couple kept themselves far from the dangers that sweep so many people downstream and try to drown them. I can guarantee that if you wait to kiss, you certainly won't be accidentally crossing sexual boundaries beforehand!

> *"For this is the will of God, your sanctification: that you should abstain from sexual immorality; that each of you should know how to possess his own vessel in **sanctification and honor**," (1 Thessalonians 4:3–4)*

You know what they say, "Practice makes perfect." The more you practice abstinence, the better you'll get at it! So should you not even touch? Well, below are some suggested guidelines to help. Remember, you've looked at the Scriptures. In the end you're accountable to God and no one else.

A Few Keys to Keep You Safe

Here's the theory: If an electric fence is put around a high voltage electric amp, it will keep those people out who cannot resist getting close from killing themselves. They may get injured, but at least they won't be electrocuted and die from the surge. This same principle is true in our lives. If we make a rule that puts a "fence" around the sinful behavior, when we are weakened and pull up close to what we know we don't want to do, we may get shocked, *but we wont get dead.* Our lives are too precious to toy with. God wants us to be whole and to live the lives He's ordained for us. After all, NO GOOD THING will He withhold from those who walk uprightly! So, if we want the good things it would behoove us to walk uprightly.

Guideline Number One:

> *". . . in which you once walked according to the course of this world, according to the prince of the power of the air, the spirit who now works in the sons of disobedience, among whom also we all once conducted ourselves in the lusts of our flesh, fulfilling the desires of the flesh and of the mind, and were by nature children of wrath, just as the others." (Ephesians 2:2, 3)*

Public places and groups are our friends. Apartments, houses, cars and even empty youth rooms are all unaccountable areas.

When no one is watching, there's danger waiting. The hardest rule I ever inflicted on myself was to not have any male in my apartment alone with me. This means even my godly male friends could not come in if they stopped by alone. Did that ever make me feel bad or just a little awkward? Yes. In fact, I didn't even like this dumb rule I made—initially. But I'd rather tell them no, and know that I'm keeping any future danger at bay. That one whom I might be tempted with isn't being singled out as "not allowed in" but as a standing rule, I never needed to face that dilemma. This was part of "foreseeing evil and hiding myself . . ." even when there didn't seem to be evil in the current situation.

Cars are not safe either. I'm not saying don't get into a car, but DO NOT hang out there. Long talks or just "being" in a car for a time is a *breeding ground* for danger (pun intended). I remember mentoring a Bible college student that was dating a good Christian guy. I was holding her accountable so I asked about the physical boundaries. She said things had been good, except when they would be in the back seat of his car. I looked at her in disbelief and asked, "What in the world are you doing in the back seat of his car?" It was so ridiculous I almost laughed. They stayed in the car to not be alone in the house, but they sat in the back to sit together. Alone is alone. Many a girl has become pregnant in a car. So, when the car goes into "park," *get out*. It saves you from having to try and enforce that decision when you no longer have the will power to be smart.

Guideline Number Two:

> *"Now concerning the things of which you wrote to me: It is good for a man not to touch a woman."*
> *(1 Corinthians 7:1)*

Physical intimacy boundaries need to be clear, and far from "sin." We discussed this earlier in the form of honoring the Lord and not simply "not sinning," but there's more to it.

When "no sex" is your only boundary, you will start building towards it little by little. You cannot be surprised when it becomes difficult to stop. It's like you're practicing for the big game, but then you're not going to go. You're rehearsing with the band every week, but you're not going to play at the gigs. It's simply silly. You start down a path, repeatedly and then say that path isn't going to take me where it's leading. You're wrong. At some point you will be sorry you even looked at that path, never mind started strolling along it.

I know more than one couple that even had "French kissing" as their physical intimacy line before marriage that have said they wished they made it stricter because our bodies are really not meant to stop there. We were created to procreate. We were meant to be intimate . . . *with our spouse.*

There was never a mechanism for intimacy with someone else, especially someone that we'd need to stop with.

The beauty of a kiss has been stolen. What once was exciting; the first touches like holding hands, are now plowed through in the rush towards intimacy. We're so very brainwashed by television and movies that dating includes everything, so waiting to kiss seems odd.

I do believe with all my heart that true physical connection should be saved for the person we are going to marry. Holding hands is about as far as I'd be willing to let myself go with someone I wasn't sure I was going to marry . . . and I mean with an engagement ring on my finger. This isn't because I'm weak, but because I want to stay strong. God has called each of us to more than ordinary. That means being willing to live differently than the ordinary person.

Guideline Number Three:

"Two are better than one, because they have a good reward for their labor. For if they fall, one will lift up his

companion. But woe to him who is alone when he falls, for he has no one to help him up. Again, if two lie down together, they will keep warm; but how can one be warm alone? Though one may be overpowered by another, two can withstand him. And a threefold cord is not quickly broken." (Ecclesiastes 4:9–12)

Accountability is necessary. Find someone of the same gender who knows your boundaries and will hold you accountable. Someone you commit to tell **every detail** to (even of your other gender friendships). This person can literally save your life. You see, when we're in the midst of situations, we can't always see what we're doing. This should be someone with whom you can be honest and who will be honest with you. This is truly critical. It's not always easy to be honest, especially if you know they might not like what you'll tell them. However, you've got to care more about BEING right than LOOKING right. You see, when you're in the midst of a situation, you'll be tempted to keep your mouth shut or only say something "if there's a problem." Nope. You need to simply keep accountable for EVERYTHING. That includes your thoughts, as well as your intentions (i.e. "I called Sarah today because I needed to know what time the Bible study was . . . although I know I could have called Sam. Not sure why, but I just noticed I like talking to her more often."). Now this doesn't mean it's a problem. You telling them doesn't define it as an issue. What you're doing is setting yourself up to make sure you don't make stupid mistakes or run ahead when you haven't yet sought the Lord. You have to be willing to listen to them and be honest with them. Ecclesiastes says, *". . . if one falls down . . ."* Don't get caught alone!

These guidelines are not for you to ponder for a future time. You cannot make these decisions AFTER you start dating. This is something you need to settle in your heart and mind—and with the Lord—before that incredible man or woman of God walks into your life. You see, no matter how much you *want* to do right, other desires and urges can take over. Your best defense is an early one. So decide now, today, what guidelines you will have in order to keep your life and heart pure before God, for yourself and your future spouse. That's what these guidelines are about: Keeping your heart and your life in tact so you can walk in the fullness of God's plan.

Satan's Tactics, Our Retaliation

> *"Therefore submit to God. Resist the devil and he will flee from you." (James 4:7)*

> *"Be sober, be vigilant; because your adversary the devil walks about like a roaring lion, seeking whom He may devour. Resist him steadfast in the faith. . ."*
> *(1 Peter 5:8, 9a)*

Satan is real. He is SEEKING to devour. He's looking for whomever he can get his claws into. If he *may* devour you, He will try. God is good to step in, to come to our aid and strengthen us. However, He also tells US to resist Satan. This isn't God's fight; it's ours. Satan is looking for weaknesses. He rarely attacks where we're strongest. Purity is an area in which most singles will have a weakness at some point. This means we need to be ready to RESIST the devil so that he must flee. God has given us the ability to resist and He expects us to exercise it.

You may have suffered under some sexual abuse in the past. It may have been when you were young or may have been more recently. Those are wounds that Satan instigated. Now he wants to exploit them. He's a fierce predator who only shows up to cause death and destruction in your life. (John 10:10) If he's already gotten away with some amount of that in the past, now is the time to stop him from any further violation. God truly wants you to be healed from those experiences, and only God—no other person or love on earth—can bring that genuine depth of healing.

Sometimes past exploitations and injuries have led to scars that seem insurmountable. Whether sexual or otherwise, Satan uses people to reach in and destroy what God intended to be a good life for us. Sometimes it is just from the leading and goading of peers or others. These pressures cause us to make poor choices. Then we end up owning those decisions as a part of us and the consequences for making them can be life altering and permanent. Instead of allowing ourselves to identify with those circumstances or poor choices, we need to recognize the author of that deception so we can instead resist His continued advances.

Satan is called a "thief." Do you realize that a thief gets away with their behavior as long as the victims are silent? If you don't report the crime, then a thief will remain free to continue stealing. Satan does that to us. He takes, and takes and we often stay silent. So he continues to use and abuse us or lead us in his own path and we follow along with the injuries still fresh in our minds and hearts, not knowing why we continue to be influenced by him. We must speak up!

There's no time like the present to deal with needed healing. Jesus never turned away a person in need. *(Even the one it looked like he was turning away, the Syro-Phoenician woman, still got her miracle because she went after it. (Mark 7)*

If there's any area in your life, especially dealing with sexual purity or emotional bondages, in which Satan has ripped you off, let's take a moment **right now** to deal with that before the Lord.

- ❖ **First: Offer up the issue or wound.** Be honest with God. He knows what you're dealing with, but if we can't be honest with Him, we're probably not being honest with ourselves. He said that when we "ask" we will be answered. This is a relationship. Ask Him for healing. Isaiah 53:5 states that Jesus' chastisement was for our "peace." God is the only One who can truly heal and transform those things that go deep. Let Him.
- ❖ **Second: Thank Him that He is faithful and will bring healing.** God says to let our requests be made known with thanksgiving. (Philippians 4:6) That means you really expect Him to answer!
- ❖ **Third: Renew your commitment to Him.** Bring your life choices to His feet. Remember, if you've truly made Him "Lord" then He's supposed to be the decision maker now.

If there's any area that you haven't surrendered to His leading, confess that right now. He wants ONLY to bless and bring healing and strength. Trust Him with that. He is a good God.

❖ **In Jesus' Name**, you can ask for all these things. First John 5:14–15 says that if we ask anything according to His will, He hears us AND if we know that He hears us, we KNOW we have the petitions we asked!
  AMEN!

You see, Satan's plot is to keep hanging guilt and shame over our heads, but when we find our freedom and release in Jesus, Satan's tactics are thwarted. He has to look elsewhere to find a hook in us. Don't only ask Jesus for forgiveness, also release that forgiveness to yourself!

SECTION FOUR

The Bigger Picture

*"Husbands, love your wives, just as Christ also loved the church and gave Himself for her, that He might sanctify and cleanse her with the washing of water by the word, that He might present her to Himself a glorious church, not having spot or wrinkle or any such thing, but that she should be holy and without blemish. So husbands ought to love their own wives as their own bodies; he who loves his wife loves himself. For no one ever hated his own flesh, but nourishes and cherishes it, just as the Lord does the church. For we are members of His body, of His flesh and of His bones. For this reason a man shall leave his father and mother and be joined to his wife, and the two shall become one flesh. This is a great mystery, but I speak concerning **Christ and the church.**" (Ephesians 5:25–32)*

I 've heard this passage somewhere close to one billion times. Ok, maybe not one billion, but probably close to one hundred million. I've heard it primarily at weddings. I've heard it also at marriage events and talks *(yes, being in ministry I'm privileged to be a part of events many people in my season of life would not participate in)*. However, I have almost never heard it clearly laid out in it's own obvious context. Let me explain. Paul exhorts husbands and wives on proper behavior, which is all well and good. Then he closes the whole section with some pretty startling comments. *"This is a great mystery, but I speak concerning Christ and the church." Wait, what? That whole passage was about Jesus and us? I certainly haven't heard too many sermons on that!*

Let me pull back to a wider scope for a moment before we delve into Paul's message here:

> *Let's go back to the Old Testament. You may have heard your pastor talk about something in the Old Testament being a "type" of Christ. He's talking about things in the Old Testament that showed us a picture of Jesus before He was born as a human. This isn't like going to the movies and seeing things that relate to Christian doctrine, but literal historical narratives that God directed through history to show us Jesus. One of the most obvious is the lamb sacrificed in the Hebrew temple sacrificial system. If you are familiar with Scripture, this won't be too difficult a question, but the answers might surprise you:*

> 1) Could the sacrificial lambs actually take away sin?

> *The answer is no. Our sins were not truly removed until Jesus came, died and was resurrected. The sacrifices showed us what was necessary, but were insufficient to fulfill it.*

> 2) What was the point of all of those sacrifices and blood if they were, on the whole, ineffectual?

> *The answer? We were being shown a picture that would, for all of history, portray what Jesus had to do, and finally accomplished for us. We see our need for a sacrifice and our inability to atone for our own sins. It also trained the Jewish people in honoring God and other important factors. However, on the whole, it was a big picture. That was its purpose.*

God often uses life situations to paint pictures. I'm not referring to us getting up in the morning and brushing our teeth. It's the children of Israel wandering through the desert for 40 years that teaches us about inheriting *(or not, as the case my be)* the promises *(or promised land)* that God has for us. It's the feeding of the 5,000 that met an actual need, but painted for us how so little can become so much. It was Peter's boldness to come to Jesus on the water, but distraction by wind and waves that pictures for us the reality of what we're capable of with Jesus, and what will happen without Him. God writes history in pictures.

Coming back to Paul's exhortation to marriage and culminating with his reference to Jesus: What is he talking about?

Did you ever notice that the church is called the Bride of Christ? In fact, the heavenly party we're going to have when this whole thing wraps up *(this whole thing meaning the earth)* is a wedding feast—Jesus' wedding feast to be exact. Well, Jesus and us. We're His bride. Paul is pointing out an incredible truth that many people miss. Righteous marriage isn't just about the married people. It's about showing a picture of Jesus and us to the world. **He's painting with us.** People ought to see married Believers and be stunned by the beauty of their relationships and interactions. How the groom gives of himself completely for his bride not worrying about protecting himself. Plus, how she submits to him in a manner that creates a unity of spirit and perspective that is neither self-deprecating nor trivial. Lived out correctly, this demonstrates that the curse that happened because of sin in Genesis 3 is now truly reversed and a unified partnership exists once again.

Paul stated, *". . . we are members of His flesh and of His bones."* That's a pretty radical statement. Here we see the concept that *one flesh* isn't just a reference to sexual intimacy, like many have thought. This is a reference to how intricately we are to be joined with one another, just as Christ and the church are. That we become so entwined with Jesus, there's no distinction between us. The language of the Bible is consistent. We're the "body" and He's the "head." We don't have a head that functions independently of its body. They work together. In fact, so much so that they aren't really referenced apart. We just refer to the whole person. Through the process of growing in Christ, WE are supposed to be continually changed more and more into HIS image. Somewhere along the way, this truth got lost from our churches and now we're just living life trying to be nice people.

Our marriages are supposed to reflect Christ and His Church . . . the way He's called us to be.

Knowing Love

If we genuinely want to have a good marriage and a solid foundation, we must know the key ingredient to the "life more abundantly" that Jesus spoke of. It's love. *We want to love and to be loved.* The truth is, however, that no one will ever love us like our Savior does. If we don't yet truly understand that love, then the love we give will be limited too.

Being loved means that we also give love. Giving love starts by getting God's love down on the inside of us. Don't blow by this topic of love thinking, 'I've got this one—*Jesus loves me, this I know*—I've known that since I was five.' We don't know. I thought I knew. The more I've studied God's love for me, the more I realize I really still don't fully get it. God is crazy about us. He loves us so much more than we know!

If you grew up in church you've possibly heard this "too many" times, but it's true. If there's one thing that is reiterated throughout the New Testament, it's that we cannot serve God or truly follow Him without walking in love. We have to learn to love—to truly love. It's different than being nice. It's not about being moral. It's about actual God-type love. Jesus summed up the entire will of God for us by saying we were to love God and love people. That's it. Simple. Right? Yes, it is simple, but not always easy. If we think, 'Yeah, I love people, that's not hard,' then we probably don't understand yet. Love is bigger than we understand . . . God-sized love is what I'm talking about.

The love of God is so deep. My first teaching assignment was to teach a class about the love of God. For six weeks, an hour each week, I went through the Bible and discussed the love of God. After doing this same class about three times I began to be convinced of one main thing: We have no idea how much God loves us. Really. I was constantly being more and more floored by how much He loves and what He's done for us. I began to feel like all I could tell the students in that hour each week was, "You're not going to get this . . . you just can't." I was overwhelmed with the time I was spending each week seeing into that love. I knew that in the one hour they couldn't grasp it . . . yet they needed to . . . I needed to . . . you need to! Ephesians 3:17 states that when we're *"rooted and grounded in love, we can know the love of Christ, which passes knowledge . . ."* Listen to that. It *"passes knowledge."* It's past finding out! So if it can't be known, then why am I trying to figure it out? How can we know the unknowable? This is how God works IN us. He takes us to places we don't understand, but IN Him, we can uncover these truths.

Have you ever seen a mother or father look at their little one and say, "I love you" and the little one looks up and says, "I love you too." Maybe you have a nephew or niece and in your times with them you tell them you love them, fully aware they do not return the same level of affection. Oh, they may think you're fun or great, or nice; but when they say, "I love you," you know it doesn't have the depth of what you feel for them. Somehow as children with child-like love, they are limited. They may love with all their hearts, but it's like their hearts aren't quite big enough to fathom the sacrificial, unending love of a parent. In their own limited way, *they do love*.

I think this is what our relationship with God looks like. We can sense His love, even know it to some degree, but we also know we don't love like He does. He looks down at us and just smiles and says, "I love you." We look, maybe roll our eyes a little and say, "Yeah, God, me too." Not even with the foggiest understanding of how MUCH He loves. It surpasses our human knowledge, but that doesn't mean it can't be understood. Knowledge isn't the way we understand the things of God. He's not trying to get hold of our minds. He wants our hearts. More specifically, He wants our spirits. That's where we can begin to understand this incredible love. That revelation comes only when we are rooted and grounded in it. To be rooted and grounded in love, we have to have the love of Christ in our heart . . . which, according to Romans 5:5, *we have*. This is such good news! *We're able to gain this understanding* . . . but it's not a simple acknowledgement. It's truly a process we need to undertake, to see who He is and how He loves. For me, it was probably about the sixth time I taught that class (that would have to be an accumulative 250-plus hours of study and focus on it), that inside of me I felt something change. Oh, I was impacted the first time and every time, but by that point, I began to *understand* the love. It felt like I was starting to truly *know* it. The key indicator: I started to love people differently. Suddenly I was more able to see how to love people, as well as how to return the love of my great God.

The Word says that we love because He first loved us. If we can love, we can do His commands. The Bible says that God is love, so if we're going to be a reflection of Him on earth, then it really comes down to love.

Can you imagine your future marriage? Does it include love? I've seen marriages that seem to be loveless. That is NOT what I will have. *I plan to be crazy in love. I'm looking forward to it.* I am eagerly anticipating my husband being crazy in love with me too! I've caught a glimpse of something crucial as I've taught about God's love. It's different from the world's version of love. The world settles for a combination of care and lust to replace love. Love isn't an emotion. Love is something we give, it's something we have, it's something we feel and something we are. Through the great leadership and mentoring I've received I'm already very aware that love in marriage isn't automatic. In fact, it has a whole lot to do with what I choose to do and whom I choose to be. I love because God first loved me. I've discovered that as long as I can love Him first, love for others is a natural outflow.

I didn't always love a lot. That may sound strange to some, but I bet many can identify with that as well. I have always cared for people, like my family or friends. People I knew. As much as I may have had affection for some, and cared for others in a more distant way, I didn't let people into my heart. I kept myself from hurt by keeping people far from me emotionally. What made it easy was that they didn't realize that I was holding back. I would let people close to me in ways that made them feel connected, even sharing personal details of my life, without ever letting them *into* my life. I didn't even realize I was doing it, but I did it nonetheless. I was accustomed to keeping people far from me and not letting their words, opinions or lives touch me. I was completely safe from harm . . . and alone. People thought they were close to me, but they didn't know my heart. No one understood me, but that was my fault. I didn't genuinely love them and I wasn't letting their love get through to me. Again, I didn't really understand I was doing this, but I had learned to barricade myself emotionally from people and I was safe and secure behind those walls . . . until the Lord began to show me (as we were digging deeper) that those walls were keeping me from genuine relationships. They would either destroy my marriage or hinder it from forming in the first place.

I felt it inside of me—that emotional detachment from others. People would say they loved me, but I simply didn't believe them. I was sure they didn't mean it. Oh, I didn't think they were lying per se. I just believed they didn't genuinely care about me in a deep way. To be honest, if I felt like they really did, I would typically start to pull back from them. My first boyfriend at age 15 told someone I was the best thing that had ever happened to him. What some girls would have thought was so very romantic thoroughly freaked me out. To my very logical mind, I thought he was either being weird or he just liked me too much! What on earth had I done to elicit that kind of response? I thought we were really good friends. What I didn't know then was that I was not able to receive love (even the 15-year-old infatuation kind of "love") because I didn't know how to love.

When the Lord began to expose this to me I wasn't really a big fan of changing it. I was safe behind those big, cold, brick walls. No one could hurt me. Then again, no one could touch me at all. I had been rejected in little ways and some big ways at various times in my early years, and somewhere along the way I determined I would be strong enough for that not to matter. People could reject me and I would be fine . . . they just couldn't get in anymore. What I didn't realize was that no one could. It was the gentle prodding of the Lord that helped me understand the outcome of this injured paradigm. I would never have a marriage of love *if I couldn't love*. If I didn't deal with this issue, the barricade I set up would forever trap me. The issue was not that I needed to love others . . . the issue was that I first needed to love God and next love and accept myself. Then I needed to trust Him to help me love and be loved by others. You see God IS love. In a sense, He can't help but love us. We, however, have the option. As I mentioned, God's love for us has been poured out in our hearts, but that doesn't mean we receive and utilize it. I have a car. That doesn't mean I drive it. It doesn't even mean I know how to drive it. I HAVE God's love in me, but that doesn't mean I give it away. I know that if I'm going to be a reflection of Him, I must love. I want to love. I needed to learn to love.

In God's ever-beautiful way, He started destroying my walls. It's funny, because I can't tell you exactly what got rid of them, yet I know it started with acknowledging them, and asking for His help. Then it was little choices, like choosing to care a little more for certain people. Even allowing myself to be vulnerable in situations as He was leading me. It was like brick-by-brick Jesus was knocking down what had been my guard to stand in that gap for me. It wasn't my job to protect me. It was His. I just needed to be obedient to stay in step with Him.

At the beginning of this chapter I said God requested us to do two things: Love God and love people. Notice what's not in this list: Getting love. With God, it's always about giving. As children we're always looking to be fair. If we give something, we want something in return. Even if we didn't give for that reason, it definitely is something that plays into how we think. It's human nature, but God's love isn't in trade. God doesn't love us because we did something right or because we love Him. Actually, it's the opposite. Romans 5:8 says, ". . . *in that while we were still sinners Christ died for us.*" That's His kind of love. He did want something from us, but it wasn't *in exchange* for His love. He just wants us. He knew that not everyone would take him up on His offer, but He did it anyway. He chose to give of Himself knowing that so many would turn their backs and choose to reject Him. He still loved, and laid down His life for us. That's God-love.

Maybe you haven't experienced that love yet. Maybe you're not even sure what that means. It's not just a story. It's not just the one-time act of love, although that's more than enough. God gives love constantly. He wants to show Himself as your loving, providing God who cares so deeply for you. If you can begin to see His love for you, you will be amazed. There's no better father, brother, friend or God than Him. He is crazy about you and me, and we get to experience that kind of love. That means we get to give that kind of love away. You will be an amazing "lover" if you can grab the truth of God's love. You can love people without expecting anything in return. You can enjoy friends and family without being frustrated if they don't live up to their end of the bargain. I'm talking about being at peace because you are loved and supplied by your God, not by the rollercoaster of support and emotion that others give.

Do you see what this will do for your marriage? You will be able to love your spouse without feeling like they "ought" to do, be, feel and act a certain way. You can give love. When they return it, it's not just an expectation, but also a precious gift. You can enjoy his or her love without demanding it. They get to "give" it to you. Can you imagine a marriage where the individuals love—act loving, give love, feel love—not out of obligation or in order to get something back, but simply because they do. They just want to love the other one. Most people enter into marriage hoping for what they may receive, but really we're only responsible for ourselves and it's about what we will **give** that proves our readiness for our wedding day.

Psalms says, *"Taste and see that the Lord is good."* (Psalm 34:8) When we get a taste of His love, we'll want more. The more of His love we experience, the more we can love others. That's God-style love. It will change the way we live and the way we love.

It was this revelation of a selfless love (instead of a selfish love) that opened my eyes to how God intended marriage to work. I began to see that if I love the Lord with all my heart, soul, mind and strength, then I can truly love someone else. *Marriage isn't about me finding someone. It's about me giving myself away to someone.* I shared this with a pastor friend of mine who has done marriage counseling longer than I've been alive and he got excited. "Tammy, that's it! You are not ready for marriage until you understand that it's about loving *them*, standing beside *them*." The picture was getting clearer. Jesus didn't come to be served, but to serve others. There is no relationship in life that God intends for us to undertake in order to boost our own ego or get something for ourselves. It's always with an attitude of giving. Still, what we get in return makes relationships so incredible. That's true about any relationship or interaction. Many people give us wisdom and support they never intended to just because they are the kind of person they are. Somehow God pours back into us when we're willing to give of ourselves. How many people do you know who come back from a missions' trip talking about how hard it was to give so much of themselves? **I've never heard it.** What people always come back saying is how changed THEY are by giving of themselves. That's what they got out of it. God's equation is that He brings blessings when we give ourselves away. Being people who love, care for and consider His body, His children, will radically transform us. In fact, Jesus said, "In as much as you did it for the least of these, you did it for Me." Wow! When we give ourselves, we give directly to Him.

Unforgiveness

There's one other overlooked and underrated thing that has the power to destroy our marriages and our lives. We dealt with the need to ask God for His forgiveness as well as forgiving ourselves for past mess-ups. The final and most critical piece is to forgive others.

Jesus gives a parable in Matthew 18 about forgiveness. The story is about a king who forgave a great debt. When that for-given person began to demand payment of a much smaller sum from someone else, the king heard and delivered him to torturers until the full original payment was made. Jesus likened this to us forgiving what others do. He makes it clear that He's forgiven the biggest debts of all, and it's our responsibility to generously give that same compassion. In fact, as we read, we understand that not forgiving leads to torture. It's not that God tortures us, but that we're delivered over to that when we allow the sin of unforgiveness to remain in our hearts.

We have all been hurt. Some of those wounds go so deep we refuse to acknowledge them for fear of opening ourselves up to the pain once again. Sometimes it's not so much the depth as the number of wounds. Growing up, there was one person who I longed to give me approval, to show me validation, and it simply never came. I retaliated and learned to protect and defend myself, but in the deepest part of me, I was wounded. I felt like I wasn't valuable or good enough. Somehow Satan twisted what was a wrong behavior from one person into what seemed like permanent damage in me.

I knew I needed to forgive. I even thought I had a few times. As years went by I felt like I had to continually forgive because I just kept getting hurt. Until one day I cried out, "I don't want to forgive anymore!" It was my humble pastor who asked me such a profound question that I was forever changed. He said, "Do you not want to forgive or do you not want to be hurt anymore?" Well, he had me there. I hated the hurt that was consistently tearing me open. If I could forgive without that side effect, I did want to forgive. I knew Jesus wanted me to forgive, but I just didn't understand how to stop the pain that seemed to come after I forgave.

The truth was that I was allowing this other person to control me. They weren't trying to. However, I was giving them that privilege. They had proven over time they were not capable of treating me well, of responding to me in kindness. This was an issue inside of them. And although I was growing by leaps and bounds in my walk with the Lord, any interaction with them tore me back down. Why? What was going on? I knew they weren't trying to, but their words pierced. I finally caught hold of this powerful truth: Forgiveness is releasing a person from their debt to you. It is not a method by which we suddenly establish what was never there.

Let me explain.

If I have a friend whom I love, who is always late, yet I ask them for a ride to the airport and well . . . wouldn't you know it . . . we're late and I miss my plane. At that time I can and would choose to forgive them. Now, does that mean I expect them to suddenly start being on time? No. That would be silly of me. Their consistent behavior has proved that they don't function by a clock. Although I love them and totally forgave them for making me late, I wouldn't suddenly expect their behavior to be different. Now, if they offer me a ride next time to "make up for it," I might accept *(but I would tell them to pick me up an hour earlier than I normally would!).*

You see, I had thought that by forgiving, not only did I wipe the slate clean of past offenses, but I also wiped it clean of past reality. Releasing forgiveness isn't about that. On the other hand, if a person has been faithful and has proven himself or herself to be honorable and then they violate the trust or mess up, forgiveness SHOULD reinstate that previous trust. At least it should to a degree that we genuinely no longer hold the violation against them.

The truth is that forgiveness is not for the other person. It's for us. It's been said, "Unforgiveness is like drinking poison and expecting someone else to die." We hold onto it because we're punishing someone else, when the truth is, we're usually the only one being damaged. This isn't something we can put off. Unforgiveness brings torture in our lives, and it destroys. This isn't just about being healthy for marriage. It's about being a healthy person now. Plus, if we learn now to release genuine forgiveness, our spouse will be so glad we did.

> ❖ Take a minute right now. Are there people you have not forgiven? Ask the Holy Spirit to bring people's names to mind and write them down. Then, don't just pray for them, but confess aloud that you do forgive them, and be specific about what that forgiveness is for. Then pray for them and tell the Lord you acknowledge they no longer have a debt to you.

The Total is the Sum of Its Parts

Living this life the way Jesus asked us to is not a small thing. Giving our lives away, releasing forgiveness, genuinely loving . . . any one of these is no small item. Yet, it is what Jesus asks of us, and **it is what marriage really requires**. In our lives we can no longer be the most important. Once married, we now give ourselves away to that person. Our personal hurts can no longer trump the need for peace and love to flow freely in the home. In a sense, it's the honest reality that it's no longer about US! *This is great training because next comes kids and THAT requires another genuine and even deeper level of selflessness!*

It's so amusing to me how many people really think this is easy or it won't be stretching . . . like, "OK, got it. I'm ready!" This kind of walk of love and forgiveness is completely opposite to our natural mindset. It literally takes intentional choices to engage our hearts in the right direction . . . to retrain our "gut response" to do things God's way instead of our own. If you're one who is a little impatient to "give yourself away," I want to warn you to be careful. Most people I've heard who feel like giving up their own life for someone else will be "easy" are people who are convinced that marriage itself will make them happier. They say they're "ready" when the truth is that marriage is their escape. If you don't like who you are now, or what life is throwing at you, getting married is certainly not the way to deal with it. That's NOT the "gift" your spouse is hoping for. Escaping into marriage will inevitably harm that relationship because it's really not an escape. It's a new journey that you bring all of YOU into.

This is why now is the time to discover yourself and to seek the Lord for His healing and His direction. No, you won't be perfect before you get married. The truth is, you just may never actually arrive at perfection *(don't be shocked, it is true)*. Yet, the more work you have done, the farther you have gone and the greater the gift you will be to your spouse and to the Kingdom of God!

A marriage is what both people bring to the table. If you are willing to grow and become more the man or woman of God you are called to be, that means God can bring the stronger man or woman to your side that He desires for you. Your part is 100% of what you're responsible for. So, while you haven't yet joined as "one flesh," work on what you've got!

A Marital Reality

Before we get to the close of this chapter on the "bigger picture," there is one marriage-related topic that is rarely addressed with singles which I think is critical to consider well before the wedding bells toll. *(Not that most of us live anywhere where churches have bells, but maybe you do.)*

It is the topic of **submission**. It's important that our own heads are clear when it comes to this very misunderstood admonition. Growing up as a Christian, it's very apparent to me now that I've studied God's Word for years that both men and women in the body of Christ are often quite confused about this topic. Many believe that "submission" to a husband is a place of degradation in one form or another. Yet, in the sight of God we are equal, so why would one spouse be punished for simply being who they are? However, submission was never meant to be about being lesser.

So then, what is "submission?"

It is not as some suppose, a place of casting aside the characteristics that make a woman unique or individual, to take on the needs and desires of a man. Many women fear submission for this very reason. They feel as though they will lose themselves, as they become a role instead of a person.

The word "submit" is "to yield oneself to the authority or will of another." That kind of action, as humans, seems frightening at worst and ludicrous at best. Why would we willingly choose to let someone else take the lead? When, in fact, we do this all the time with our bosses, coworkers, even our friends and others we interact with. We choose to let another's opinion or their will pick the restaurant where we eat or instruct us as to what clothes look good on us. In any partnership, some level of submission is going on continually.

The biblical definition of "submission" is almost always drawn out of the passages where Paul instructs submission to husbands. However, submission is defined more clearly when we look at it throughout Scripture. God's wisdom through Solomon in Proverbs *(though not a man that chose wisely when it came to women, but we'll not focus on that)* will actually help us unlock an understanding of what submission is really all about.

> *". . . the contentions of a wife are a continual dripping (irritation). . . a prudent wife is from the Lord." (Proverbs 19:13–14)*

Solomon clarifies two possible characteristics of a wife: prudent or contentious.

In verse 14, Solomon says, "A prudent wife is from the Lord." That means she is a gift. Look up the word prudent and you might be surprised. It isn't a woman who dresses modestly and wears her hair in a bun. A "prudent" woman is one who is "marked by wisdom or judiciousness" and is "shrewd in the management of practical affairs." Now you might think, 'Wait, if she's submissive, she doesn't need to be "shrewd in management" or really wise, because that's what her husband is for.' *You would be wrong*. Does your boss expect you to wait on him or her for every decision you make? Does he or she wait for your suggestions or thoughts and then make every decision for the company by him or herself? If so, you may need a new job. A good leader is only as good as the team they are a part of. If you are on that team, it is because of your insight and input, not because of your ability to agree with the boss no matter what.

Look at verse 13 now. Solomon says what a contentious wife is . . . *irritating*! What is "contentious?" Well, it's not someone you want to be around. A contentious person is one who brings in strife. The contentious person is trying to win an argument instead of trying to solve a matter. A synonym for "contention" is "discord." This word gives a wonderful picture for marriage when we look at the musical definition. Discord is "a combination of musical sounds that strikes the ear harshly." In music there are two basic ways for singers or instruments to create a pleasant sound.

The first is to sing or play the melody together. This gives a strong lead to those who would follow or join in. The sound is clear and the direction apparent. The second is for one to sing or play the melody while the other is in harmony. This time the two musicians are working in different ways with different notes, but mixing to create a new sound. This time a richer sound with more variation is produced. Each of these has their place and use within music. However, never do you want to come to a place of dissonance or discord. This means the people who were making music together are creating a harsh sound that no one wants to hear. Maybe the musicians are both trying to lead, or maybe they just chose to do their own thing because they thought they knew best. Either way, the sound produced is unpleasant and no one can understand or follow what is going on.

Marriage is exactly the same. If the two parties can agree and sing the same notes (so to speak), a strong lead is created, that their children can follow and that their hearts can agree together upon. If they are able to harmonize, then a rich outflow of both people's strengths is created. However, harmony isn't possible if it isn't clear who is supposed to sing the melody. If both people try to take the lead, there is no clear direction, and quickly dissonance instead of harmony (or contention instead of unity) is established. That's not pleasant for those around or for those involved. A marriage relationship needs clarity in order to make music.

So, did God intend that the man always sing the lead? No. If God truly established male leadership as the only option in every situation, then He could **never** go against that truth. If that was the case, not one biblical example should be available to prove otherwise, yet there is. The first clear picture is in the Book of Judges (in the Old Testament) with the judge, Deborah. She was the leader of all Israel. People came to her to establish justice in the land and she led powerfully by God's direction. She was a married woman. Her leadership of the nation was while in submission to her husband. Is that possible? Yes. It isn't by coincidence that God wrote:

> *"Now Deborah, a prophetess, **the wife of Lapidoth**, was judging Israel at that time." (Judges 4:4, NKJV)*

She was clearly "the wife of." She was not acting as an independent person. Yet in her position, she was obviously the one people came to, not her husband. She was the judge of Israel.

When God established marriage, He said, *". . . the two shall become one flesh."* This was not in order for the parties to abandon all personal traits or lose their individuality, but a mutual union wherein the two actually join together. It truly is a mystery how God created it to be. This is why God is so specific about how marriage is supposed to work. It is also the reason that Satan has worked so hard to make sure that sin (premarital sex, sexual satisfaction without your marriage partner, same-sex relationships) contaminates the truth of God's plan. Now when people want to build a righteous marriage, there are so many mixed signals that many start making up their own rules about marriage, regardless of what God says. God's intention for marriage was a complimentary partnership. Adam and Eve were created *together* as a complete unit in the image of God. They were given dominion *together* over the earth. The intent was a partnership, but sin got in the way. It is now up to the people of God to live free of the consequences of that fall (Genesis 3:14–19) and show the world how marriage was meant to be. Christ has redeemed us and so we ought to live!

It is important to recognize that submission itself has more to do with harmony than with being a follower. We often get the picture in our mind that sub*mitting* is because women are substandard, or "less than." Instead consider it this way: A wife is sub*stantial* and absolutely necessary to complete the work God has in store for both husband and wife. Her part of the song is crucial to it coming out clearly. She is no less valuable or less prominent in His plan. However God has required that she allow her husband to take the lead in their relationship. That doesn't mean he always is in front in everything and every way. Each couple has different personalities and realities they're dealing with. What it does require is a willing heart from women to trust God enough that you are willing to submit to your husband, even when you think he's wrong.

The mandate on the husband is equally impressive: To love her as Christ loved the church and gave Himself for her. Jesus is the example. He has given up everything for His bride. His delight is in bringing joy to His people. Never has Christ tried to take our individuality away, but instead fosters an atmosphere for unity and self-sacrifice. He doesn't lead as though the Church ought to be mindless drones. He wants us to grow and become powerful and effective. Christ is not intimidated by the possibility of us outshining Him. He knows that the brighter we shine; it is truly His body gaining recognition. Husbands need to see this. For a wife to shine, the spotlight she may receive cannot intimidate her husband. He should glory in that, knowing that they are one flesh and it is a spotlight ultimately on them and on the Lord.

Conversely, the wife cannot feel that when her husband soars, she is stuck in the nest or behind the scenes, but instead she should realize that he is able to soar because of the encouragement and strength that has been created through their partnership.

When Paul said (by inspiration of the Holy Spirit),

> *"Wives, submit to your own husbands, as is fitting in the Lord." (Colossians 3:18)*

And again . . .

> *"Wives, submit to your own husbands, as to the Lord." (Ephesians 5:22)*

He was not making a suggestion, but stating a command from the Lord. Although it is easy to see why some could at times look at these passages alone and think they are unfair or not balanced, there's more to it. Notice God didn't mandate at creation that women are naturally mindless and can't make decisions or that they would be desperate creations looking for a man. On the contrary, as we saw in Proverbs chapter 19, a husband should look for a wife that is wise. In fact, in the last chapter of the book of Proverbs, Solomon points out the incredible asset that a wife who is tenacious and shrewd in business can be. The point is that wives ought to be strong, smart *and* submissive. For too long the myth has been propagated that those characteristics cannot coexist. It is time for women of God to rise to the challenge and men of God to validate them. Jesus said in Mark 10:44–45,

> *". . . whoever of you desires to be first shall be slave of all. For even the Son of Man did not come to be served, but to serve, and to give His life a ransom for many."*

To be a woman of God and a godly wife is a high calling. To be a man of God and a godly husband is not an easy path. Yet, too many of us do not believe these words of Jesus. If we did, we would not be afraid to serve one another. We wouldn't be scared of working in the shadows when called upon. Jesus Himself said

He came to serve. He was not always in the background, hidden from view. Conversely He was not always in the limelight. **He is our example**. Whether called to a public stage or the platform in the home (or a mixture of the two), no one should fear being who Jesus has called him or her to be. His love for each one of us runs deeper than we can comprehend. It is critical that men and women both see that the Lord is not looking to hide His precious girls in the dark, but to help them shine in His kingdom. It brings Him glory and honor for His daughters to shine.

> *"Do not fear, little flock, for it is your Father's good pleasure to give you the kingdom. Sell what you have and give alms; provide yourselves money bags which do not grow old, a treasure in the heavens that does not fail, where no thief approaches nor moth destroys. For where your treasure is, there your heart will be also." (Luke 12:32–34)*

Father doesn't want us to worry about what we should eat, what we should drink, or even how to protect our status. He is in love with us. He wants to see us blessed and happy. We need to stop letting fear keep us from God's commands. Fear will keep us from the life of fulfillment and joy He intended. The life that will set us free because it is based on His truth. Whether male or female, that is the life we are called to live: A life of service. That is the life where we will find joy, peace and hope. It is the life of Christ.

Arranged Marriages?

According to Ephesians 2:10, God has planned out good works for us to accomplish. Have you ever wondered how that relates to WHO ends up as our spouse? I guess the question is, if God was able to truly lead and guide us fully (because we fully surrender to Him), would we end up with someone different than if we just chose for ourselves? How would it all work if He really got to do it His way? I wondered. I wanted to know how to find the *right person* . . . or if there really was a "right" person. My curiosity was piqued when I was still in high school, and it was one of those questions everyone had a "theory" on, but I wanted to "know."

I knew the story of my parents: A blind date through mutual friends and how they "knew." Knew what? I assumed that meant that they knew it was God's plan for them to come together. It seemed to sound right. Two people meet, recognize God's plan is for them to be together, and get married. Of course, this theory has a few problems. One obvious challenge is that many people don't know God. In which case, do they *always* marry the wrong person? Also, what about those people who know God, but don't really listen to Him all that much? Do they *never* get it right?

This quest for understanding is part of what impacted my decision not to "date around" any more when I was younger. I wanted to do this God's way, not my own. I even read a book about life and relationships and the authors said that they believed God blessed their relationships and made them work. They stated that it's not a matter of "the right one," but a matter of making the right choices with the one you are with. Well, that made good sense. After all, if you are married, that HAS to be the right one *(at least now it is!)*. So, I basically believed that perspective, although I still believe God is more intentional than that. As I look at Scripture, I just don't see a God who blesses by happenstance. The one verse that always struck me was in Paul's missionary journeys when he was going to go preach the gospel in another city, but it says, *"the Spirit did not permit them"* (Acts 16:7). The very thought of the Holy Spirit not wanting to get the gospel somewhere makes NO logical sense. But when we understand how God operates in Divine appointments and that "to everything there is a season . . ." we realize that our own understanding is very limited. It's a simple fact that we have to be dependent on God. In fact, that's where true humility comes from—an understanding of our dependency on Him. It was my gradual realization of my dependency on Him that started taking me down the path of further understanding on this topic.

From the beginning, God has never been "hands off." Christian culture talks this way sometimes, but that's not the image of God we see in the Bible. He placed man and woman together in the garden and had a plan. Then He told us how much He loves us and that He knew us before we were even born (Jeremiah 1:5). He "formed" us in our mother's womb (Isaiah 44:2). Then in the New Testament He told us He prepared *"good works beforehand that we should walk in them."* In other words, He's got things in mind and in store for us, **if** we choose to walk His way. If He's done all this, and knows everything about me, and has an incredible plan for me, how is it possible that He doesn't even know whom I *should* be with for the rest of my life? Even more, wouldn't He be preparing someone for me and me for someone, if we were submitted to Him? After searching Scripture, any alternative didn't make sense.

I understand the arguments that come from logic. After all, if there's just one person for each of us, what if we're not paying attention to God when we get married? Are we bound to the "wrong" one, till death do us part? Plus, if there's only one, does that mean when someone dies, there's a person out there who will never get married? This isn't the kind of logic that helps us understand God. I don't think it has anything to do with there being "one" person, it's about letting God choose the "best" one for each of us. Think of it this way: At any point in our lives we could get married, in each season. Based on various choices, we'll be in a different place in our life journey. Now, let's just say that had we walked with God at age 18, we might have had a perfect mate show up, but instead we walked in rebellion and didn't turn it around until we were 22. Now, based on our life struggles and situations, the perfect mate might not be that same person. However, it really doesn't matter, *because God is omniscient. He knows everything to begin with*. He knows what choices we will make and those we won't. In fact, Scripture tells us we're predestined to know Him *according to His foreknowledge*! In other words we have a free choice, but it's because of His knowledge of our choices that we are also predestined. It's not an *either/or* proposition, but *both*. So, He knows when we will choose right, or wrong. This is the beauty of following Him, because even when we mess up, He's not thrown off by it and already has the way to turn things back around. He's ready for whatever we throw at Him. He's a good God. He loves us. So, is there a *right* one? The question is really: <u>Does He know the *best* one, and the *best* timing</u>

for marriage? I don't see how you can't answer, "Yes. Absolutely." If we will seek Him, He has just the right spouse for each of us.

This is the most significant decision of our lives besides making Jesus our Lord. God's not just tossing the ball into our court, saying, "Go figure it out." Even in the Old Testament we see glimmers of God-reality in this arena. Abraham sent a servant to find a wife for his son, Isaac. When the servant came to the village he was looking for, his prayer was this:

> *"Now let it be that the young woman to whom I say, 'Please let down your pitcher that I may drink,' and she says, 'Drink, and I will also give your camels a drink'; let her be the one **You have appointed for Your servant Isaac**. And by this I will know that You have shown kindness to my master." (Genesis 24:14)*

And so it was. Rebekah was the one. What was the result?

> *"Then Isaac brought her into his mother Sarah's tent . . . and she became his wife, and he loved her . . ." (Genesis 24:67)*

Even in this Old Testament reality, when God was sought for the spouse, the result was love. The Holy Spirit didn't need to include that in the story. After all, it was normal back then for marriage to be of practicality, not love. And this wasn't even a marriage that either one had a real say in, yet "he loved her" right from the start. *God is just that good.*

To our modern minds, the concept of arranged marriage is not only archaic, but also even abusive. In fact, it can be both. However, let's pull back to the theory *behind* arranged marriages. The concept is that a father, who wants what's best for his daughter and is much more aware of the ways of the world is able to contract a marriage to someone that is proven to be able to provide for her and, from his perspective, will make her happy. Unfortunately, when dealing with humans, our view of these things is very limited, thus the reason for many unhappy arranged marriages. If we put Father God in that spot . . . well, now we're looking at a very different picture. He does know what is best for both parties and He does know what would make them both happy. In fact, He desires the marriage to flourish and be blessed even more than the others involved. Why can't we trust Him in that?

In a sense what I'm saying is that I believe in arranged marriage. I'm just very particular about **Who** does the arranging.

Picture a wedding. As the bride reaches the end of the aisle, her father leans over and kisses her cheek and "gives her away" to her husband. The picture is of the one who has been entrusted with her care and protection handing her over to another who will do the same.

Whether male or female, this is a picture of our Father God. He first wants all of us. To know that we trust Him fully with our care and protection; that He holds our heart. He wants to join us together with just the right person, and when He selects the time to "give us away" **it's His role to give us**, joining us to just the right one. He will give us away, whole and unbroken to *become one* in that new union.

Many people have gotten married outside of God's will and missed out on much of the blessing that God had for them. However, God is a restorer. That means even when we miss it, He doesn't. So what happens if someone gets married and then realizes they should have waited, or listened to God? Is it too late? It's too late to do it right from the start, but it's never too late to start fresh today. Although that couple is in a tougher spot, God will always honor the marriage covenant. That means once we've entered into that covenant, he or she is now God's chosen for us. However, those people do have the opportunity to submit their lives to Him, and let Him make that relationship, not just right, but the best choice now. This restoration process is a blessing from God. We can always stand firm that He will make a way! What I want you to realize, however, is that in these situations often both people don't want the same things; to be on the same path that God wants. Then it's a much more difficult walk. Singles, this is our choice. We can pick for ourselves and ask God to fix it, or we can wait and let Him bring us the right one to begin with.

I know what I'm choosing.

SECTION FIVE

What Now?

*N*ow what? So, I work on these important things, change my paradigm and then God will send me a spouse?

Not so fast my friend. The point of walking out this life isn't about how to get to the altar. It's about being right before the Lord. It's about discovering His life and the abundance He promises. This is a walk of faith. It takes patience, and it will take trust—trust that He really will come through—and patience to see His desired outcome. Trust that we can't do it on our own, and patience to keep our hearts from jumping ahead.

In the New Testament, the patriarch of Israel, Abraham, is called, *the father of faith.* God promised him a son by his wife Sarah and he waited 25 years for that promise to be fulfilled. He definitely tried to work it out in other ways, but it was actually 12 years before he even tried a Plan B! That's impressive since most of us can't wait one year without being frustrated and taking matters into our own hands. Even in his disobedience, never did that change what God had in mind for him, nor what God was willing to do for him. Eventually he got his promised son.

Getting God's best for **anything** takes patience. Abraham was promised a son, and it took 25 years. It doesn't always take that long (in fact, rarely!), but we can't expect His promises to come to pass immediately. A promise from God will definitely come if we will wait confidently, expecting Him to be true to His word. He knows the desires of our heart and the variables of what seems to us as an uncertain future.

Let's look back again at Abraham and the faith he had to carry him through. The faith he had was pretty incredible.

> *"By faith Abraham, when he was tested, offered up Isaac and he who had received the promises offered up his only begotten son ˙... concluding that God was able to raise him up, even from the dead..."*
> *(Hebrews 11: 17–19)*

Abraham's faith was proven when he was willing to give up the very thing God promised him. Most people make comments like "faith without works is dead" *(referring to James 2:20)* and then associate those works with working towards the goal of obtaining their promise. However, in that same passage in the Book of James, he refers back to this story of Abraham, saying that it was THIS work that proved Abraham's faith. His faith was so strong, that even God's instruction to destroy what God had given him (his own child!) was not enough to deter Abraham from expecting God to come through anyway!

A powerful minister I know told me about how the Lord had prompted her that the guy she was dating would be her husband. She was quite excited and although they hadn't necessarily discussed marriage yet, she was very confident. Then they broke up. They got back together and broke up again. She was so confused. She was sure she had heard the Lord, but at the same time after the last break-up, she felt that the Lord was telling her to give it up and release the relationship completely. She said it felt like Isaac on that altar. The promise she had believed God for, for years, He was suddenly asking her to release. In tears, she did. And soon after that, he left town. She was distraught. Yet, a few weeks later he returned, and they not only got back together, but the Lord had dealt with the issues going on in his heart during that time, and he returned ready to propose. They are now happily married with a handful of fabulous kids.

Something happens when we are willing to wait on God. Something happened to Abraham during those 25 years of waiting. Something changed inside of him. Somehow holding onto God became more important than holding onto the "thing" God gave him. It was more important that he obey. It was more important that my minister friend do what God was asking of her.

Somehow in that release came the ultimate blessing. They couldn't have known what the exact outcome would be; yet they obeyed. This is what a true walk of faith looks like.

> *". . . but imitate those who through faith and patience inherit the promises." (Hebrews 6:12)*

If you already desire to be married *(or wish you were already married)*, it's important to take time to align your perspective with God's. Reread the passages of Scripture I've outlined, or portions of this book that speak God's truth in a way you'd previously not considered. Hearing something once does not mean our minds and hearts have grasped it. In the first section, I listed quite a few verses that speak to the total goodness of how God is toward His kids. Simply meditating on those verses could change your whole life. That is priority number one. We will not tap into God's unlimited goodness without renewing our minds to the REALITY of who He truly is.

Second, you need to consider this question: **Would you sacrifice having the abundant life God promised in order to have a spouse?** I know those don't necessarily oppose one another, but you need to be able to answer the question. One of the reasons people end up in bad marriages, or at least unhappy ones, is because they chose "being married" over "waiting on God." If you recognize that these two things CAN be in opposition, then you won't be so quick to think the next "good Christian" option that heads your way MUST be God's choice for you. It's happened to more than one person and you need to determine in your heart, and with your words before the Lord, that it won't be you.

A dear lady I've known since I was a child told me how she married when she was very young. When they were dating, he would quote Scripture and treated her like a queen. She can now admit that though she'd known him for a while, she hadn't really gotten to know him outside of their dating sphere. In other words, she only experienced the man he wanted her to see. He seemed like a good man, but that façade quickly faded once they were married and she endured rape and beatings that had her eventually fighting for her life. I'm not sharing this because I'm suggesting that if you marry the wrong person you'll endure hell on earth. However, I do want to reiterate the fact that **we are not omniscient**. We do not make the best choices for ourselves, and what seems like a good idea to us is often more dangerous than we could ever imagine. We have to be people who know God's voice and who obey Him. This is also why God brings others into our lives to help us along the way. I often warn people that if you typically trust someone—a pastor, leader, older friend, mentor or family member, but they do not agree with the person you bring home as a potential mate: Beware! Your emotions may say otherwise, but there's a reason why you've always trusted that person.

The reality is that sometimes we look at our options as: 1) Get married soon; or 2) Get married later. Well, if you think the two options are equal, that is an easy choice. The problem is that the options are not always equal. They look a little more like this: 1) A more difficult marriage sooner; or 2) A more fulfilled and stronger marriage that I have to wait for. You may think, *"C'mon! It isn't always more difficult."* That's very true. Often God brings couples together very early in life. I'm not against getting married at an early age. Remember what we're talking about—marriage being the focus. Trust me, if your focus is to be married, and not to put God first and please Him, your marriage will MOST DEFINITELY be more difficult. Your focus must be to follow fully after what God is calling you to.

Why am I passionate about this? Well, first because I want the best God has for me. Second, however, is because I believe that the body of Christ has been lulled into accepting second-rate Christianity for too long. God wants better for us. God wants His best for us.

I've seen the most "in love" Christian couples end up filing for divorce in less than five years. Why? Ask them, they'll tell you. They wanted "marriage." Once that becomes the focus and goal, it gets in the way of God developing "marriage" into us. Being married is a life-long commitment. It takes more of our life than any occupation or passion. Sure, we can figure it out along the way. Or we can let God work it in us before we walk down the aisle. We wouldn't learn to do surgery by cutting open family members. We would study and prepare and then even practice before operating on someone we love *(or hopefully on anyone!)*. Marriage shouldn't be treated with less care. We must remember that getting married isn't the end. Getting married is the start of a shared life, a change from what we've known so far. Let God get you ready for that adventure. Let Him change you now, strengthen you now, refine you now. It's time that His children started to trust Him. Let God have His perfect work in you.

Your Job

You may already know what your "calling" is. What you're going "to be." You may already feel like you're well on your way toward that "ultimate" place. On the other hand, you may have no idea of anything beyond the job you currently hold. Perhaps what God wants hasn't really been a factor so far. Maybe you just haven't known how to find that out. Either way, you do have a calling. It's in THAT Divine purpose for your life that God can release your potential and you will find the greatest fulfillment.

> *"And He gave some to be apostles, some prophets, some evangelists and some pastors and teachers, for the **equipping of the saints for the work of ministry** . . ."* *(Ephesians 4:11)*

> *". . . the whole body, joined and knit together by what **every** joint supplies, according to the effective working by which every part does its share, causes growth . . ."* *(Ephesians 4:16)*

You may not know this, but every Christian has a calling. At the beginning of this same passage in Ephesians, Paul talks about "walking worthy of the calling with which YOU were called." He wasn't speaking to pastors, but to the church. Every believer is called. In fact, when we read verse 11, there's a pretty stark contrast to what we've typically believed. Pastors and prophets, and those we would call "ministers" are the ones who are called to help US do the work of ministry. They aren't the ones responsible to fulfill God's entire mandate on the earth. Instead, they are gifts to the Body so that WE can fulfill God's mandate on the earth. Our purpose for living is not our job—it's our calling. Now those two things could be very intertwined, but consider this: What if no one ever paid you to do what you're called to do? Would you still do it? Jesus said it this way, ". . . I must be about My Father's business." Our primary job on the earth is to be about what matters to Him. Your job will probably not be in a church or *ministry* field. That's does not define your calling. God is asking if we'll hear Him and participate in His calling, His agenda. Our job title is insignificant if we are truly fulfilling the ministry He is calling us to. God has a lot to get accomplished on this earth and He needs all of His children to be committed to making it happen. *We are all called to ministry.*

The wonderful thing about serving God is that it's rarely dull. If you're bored I can almost guarantee that you're either not where you should be or He's about to move you *(the other option is that He's testing your faithfulness . . . you definitely want to pass that test, or it will be more of the same in the future).* The Lord does not only want to accomplish something *through* us, but also *in* us. Our role in church is part of that calling. Maybe you're serving in the nursery at church. Possibly you help by handing out food through a local mission. The part you play is just one piece of the puzzle God is orchestrating that makes up your life. What if you're supposed to be helping in a ministry, but you just feel like you don't have the time or you keep putting it off? The result? You may never know. It could have been someone in there that you prayed for who would have been healed. It could have been that your spouse would walk through those doors. Or it could have been that some of the good training and teaching God wanted to do in you through experience was short-changed because you didn't think you were really "called."

What it really comes down to . . . not just ministry, but in everything . . . is that God wants your heart. He desires to be the Lord of your life in a tangible way. He wants to know that your whole existence is wrapped in your commitment to Him. He isn't just looking for your service, but your service is an expression of your willingness to obey. Positions and roles are not the keys. It's how we serve Him and whom we are becoming along the way that matters. You may not see it this way, but your role in your local church is a high calling. Teaching two- and three-year-olds about God's love, while their parents are also being ministered to is a beautiful expression of God's love. Cleaning up the bathrooms so that people aren't offended or feel awkward coming to church is a precious act of service in God's eyes. Ask the Lord what part to play. If you're not sure, just start. You cannot go wrong in serving. Whatever your role, do not take it lightly. God sees and smiles when His kids take on the family business.

As we wholeheartedly serve God, our heart of loyalty to His plan will become the most attractive thing about us. Our devotion to God will easily spill over into other areas of our life. As God brings us together with our spouse, she or he will be able to trust us easily, because we are a trustworthy person. Doubts that can hinder a married couple's intimacy will be eliminated because of the honesty and integrity of our life. In a sense, because we have chosen to stay faithful to God, we have then chosen to stay faithful to our spouse . . . even before we knew them! The trust and faith between us will be explosive.

I have sensed in my heart that the Day of the Lord draws near. God is calling His children back to an intimacy with Him that most Christians have never experienced. I believe that is why He is stirring His children to wait on Him more and more for guidance and instruction. He wants to bring us into marriages that are whole and fulfilling. *Enough is enough* of us doing things the way the rest of the world behaves. His children are supposed to have it better! That is what He's calling us to. He wants us to do things differently, to bring about different results.

In Proverbs, Solomon writes about marriage and love in a way we imagine, but don't always see, to "*. . . always be enraptured with her love.*" (Proverbs 5:19) A marriage, where both people are satisfied and fully enraptured in their love, is not even like what the fictionalized versions of love we see on TV are like. This is different than most marriages I've ever seen. Here Solomon wrote to "**always** be enraptured . . ." That's a long-term commitment—knowing that our spouse is THE one for us—forever. Not just that we've *decided* that, but we're *excited* about it. This doesn't happen out of desire. This is something only God can make endure.

I'll admit one of the best things that ever happened for me was when I actually saw "proof" of what the Lord had been stirring in me as His reality for marriage. It was through a couple that served in ministry together. These pastors became close friends. Both are strong leaders, both are filled with God's love and yet they are also both very human. The more I was around them and their kids, the more I noticed they genuinely spoke to each other with respect, even in tense moments. While spending time at their home I observed that they were both willing to repent when things got heated *(because, even in great marriages, disagreements still happen)*. However, what shocked me was that in the end it was as though neither was trying to win. They tried to listen, not only to each other, but also to their children. Though there were certainly mistakes and issues, I saw so much genuine love for each other I was forever changed. They demonstrated what God's will for marriage is. Not by being perfect, but by being submitted to God and humble enough to admit mistakes. I am forever ruined to the idea of a marriage that is an imbalanced emotional rollercoaster.

I discovered some of their story and though they were only a few years out of high school when they married, they had both been intent on listening to the Lord for His direction in marriage. In fact, each had stories of God rescuing them from a previously intended-for-marriage relationship because they listened to Him. Now over 20 years later, they are genuinely more like best friends than most couples I've ever met—and both of them are fulfilling their callings.

It's the realities I see in Scripture and the images God has shown to me on this earth that keep me from being influenced when people say things to me like, "Tammy, don't be so picky, no one is perfect." It's amusing to me that their perception of my singleness is because I'm picky. I don't know where they would gather that. *I'm not turning down proposals left and right.* However, it's easy to misunderstand that just because I have said "no" when others would say, "let's see," that I am somehow being picky. I think I'm pretty NOT picky when it comes to men, but *I am picky* when it comes to my life. I'm bent on only allowing God's best. I don't always do it right, but I'm sure trying by His grace. This doesn't mean I'm convinced that the moment I meet "Mr. Right" I'm going to "know" and everything will just fall into place. However, it does mean that I refuse to try out a bunch of Mr. Wrongs just hoping God will keep me from making a mistake. That just sounds foolish . . . *and exhausting.*

Others who hear me talk about marriage say things like, "Well, marriage is hard work," insinuating that my view of marriage is too rose-colored. I suppose I can accept that. I'm a content person. God has helped me through some very difficult seasons, and I just don't believe that He's going to throw me into the deep end and shout, "Paddle!" Yes, marriage, kids, LIFE takes hard work! The difference is that I expect the work to bring results.

I've not only seen proof, but now I *am* proof. I've seen how my God is well able *and* very willing to work on my behalf. I've also discovered that for years I was following Him with good intentions, but it wasn't a personal ongoing relationship. What I have with Him now makes all the difference in the world.

What is my vision of marriage? Well, I see myself in a fun marriage. I see myself in a relationship that is filled with enjoyment. I see a marriage that is consummated on our wedding night. I see a friendship that can stand the test of time; and a partnership that no person can break down or come between. Above all, I see a passion for God and each other that shines to everyone around us. I see a picture of Christ and the church.

Can you see that for yourself? Genuine enjoyment until death parts you? That's the marriage I will have. I've committed to it. I expect it. I'm excited about it. What will you expect?

Thanksgiving Victory

An important key that will unlock your joy and bring you closer to the Lord is in Philippians 4:6 where it says, *". . . Be anxious for nothing, but in everything by prayer and supplication, with thanksgiving, let your requests be made known to God."* Many believers don't really understand this concept. We present our requests, with longing and discouragement, and then say "thank you" as though we "paired it" with *thanksgiving* and thereby fulfilled what this verse is asking of us *(Helpful hint: If you're praying in misery, then you're not praying with thanksgiving . . . Just in case you weren't aware.).*

An abundant life, the good life that has Jesus at the center of it, is a life that thanksgiving naturally flows out of. The awareness that God IS actually good. That He actually wants to fulfill His plan in your life. That you are precious to Him and He will come to your aid, your rescue and be your strength is clear. When presenting requests to Him there is thanksgiving in your heart. You will have gratefulness for the good that He has done. Thanks for the breath in your lungs and the gift of salvation. On top of that, there's a deep-rooted awareness that He will come through. He's on your side. So when you ask, you aren't begging. You don't come with a forlorn expression hoping that maybe God would be so benevolent as to grant your petition. In fact, the Lord even instructs us to *"come BOLDLY!"* to His throne. (Hebrews 4:16)

We aren't just sinners anymore. We can't identify constantly with the old nature or we'll be stuck in "not worthy" mode and even resist the good things He wants for us. Yes, we do sin and we do mess up. No, we are not "sinners" in God's eyes any longer. We are redeemed and when we sin, all we have to do is confess it and it's wiped completely 100% away, never to be addressed again. That's the incredible relationship we have with God! We need to grab hold of this relationship and walk it out. Imagine telling your kids, "I got a cheesecake, it's in the kitchen, and you can help yourselves." Then, one of your children comes to you a few hours later with sorrowful eyes, asking if they could have just a small piece. I don't know about you, but I'd be a little confused. *Didn't I already say you could?* Maybe they hadn't cleaned their room or maybe they just assumed that wasn't for them. Whatever the case they opted out of the good stuff. Now imagine your child telling others that you never get them anything special and they have a hard life. I don't know about you, but that would frustrate me. The truth is, this is how we treat God sometimes . . . *and He's done a lot better than cheesecake.*

So come boldly and come with thanksgiving! How much better it is to imagine seeing your child chomping down that piece of cheesecake and serving their siblings with a huge smile and a big, "Thanks Mom and Dad!" Just thinking of that would make **you** smile. If you can see how to be a good parent, why do you think God isn't? He wants to show us His goodness.

In Philippians, He asks us to make our requests **with** thanksgiving. That means before we get the cheesecake, we're thankful. How does that work? Well, let's pull this back around to what we're focusing on: Marriage. When we talk to God about our future spouse, do we expect that He's listening? Do we believe He wants to fulfill the desires of our heart? If so, when we're praying, we know He's saying, "Yes." And when God says, "Yes," we should say "Thank you!"

I pray for my husband. The one I haven't met *(as far as I know)*. I don't just pray for him to come, I pray FOR him. He's a real person and God wants to do great things through him. Just because I don't know who He is, doesn't mean that God is unsure. So I pray for him, for his strength and protection. I pray because I really believe that God knows exactly who he is, even if I don't. I pray because I expect God to hear me and to act according to what He's said in His Word. I pray with thanksgiving that we will be together and we will be happy. I thank God because I trust Him completely. When we're thankful, we can't be unhappy.

Try it. It works—prayer and thanksgiving. Expect your relationship with God to be one that lives and grows. Expect that God is who He said He would be in His Word. It honors Him when we take Him at His Word. If we can get thanks out of our mouth on a regular basis, we will find a smile on our face just a little more often. Thank God now for the spouse He has for you. Thank Him that he or she is safe and blessed. Thank Him that He's bringing the two of you to intersect in His perfect timing. Thank Him that your life today is fulfilling (even if you're struggling with it) and that you will have joy today. Thank Him that He's faithful and that you belong to Him.

Starting With Today

So, today you are still single.

Today, cast your cares on Him, because He cares for you. God already knows whom you will marry, how many kids you will have and how many freckles will be on their precious faces. That is not something you need to consider today. Today is the day to commit your life afresh to God's plan. He has called you to have a role in His kingdom. There is so much He desires to accomplish on this earth—*and especially through you!*

God loves you so very much and He wants to spend time with you each day. He wants to show you things to come. He wants to bless your life. He wants to bring peace and joy into your heart like you've never experienced before. Today is the day to start. If you're in a place where you've never fully given your life to Jesus, today is the day for that! He loves you and wants to show you His goodness. It's so simple to start (or start fresh) with Him.

> Simply speak to Father God in prayer right now. Tell Him you need Him, that you are grateful for His goodness and His plans for your life. (Ephesians 2:10) Thank Him for the sacrifice that Jesus made for your sin (John 3:16) and ask for forgiveness and to be fully made new. We always ask *in Jesus' name* (John 14:13) and—*Amen!*

If you're serious about living life God's way, then I want to share some helpful tips to launch into this journey (or refresh it a bit for optimal results):

1) **Get on a regular Bible reading schedule.** To know God you need to know His word, not just about it. Reading just a chapter or two a day can make a big difference if you just ask the Holy Spirit to open your eyes. God will reveal Himself to you!

2) **Pray.** God wants to talk with you in a two-way conversation. It's not as intimidating as you might think. Just talk to Him, ask for His wisdom. Keep a journal handy to write down what you sense is the way He's leading you. A journal is also a great place to keep notes about the things you read in the Bible each day and what God showed you through them.

3) **Be part of a church that challenges you to grow.** Be sure to attend EACH WEEK and even mid-week services, listening to what is being said and truly trying to apply it in your daily life. Sermons are meant to be life changing, not forgotten.

4) **Get involved at church.** The Body of Christ is made up of many members and that includes you. A man or woman of God is involved in His ministry and can be counted on.

5) **Get an accountability partner.** Find someone you can talk to about the things of God, and who will commit to asking the tough questions about your life, your thought life and your integrity. Plus, someone who can hold you accountable to be reading the Bible regularly.

These are really simple steps, but most of us don't consistently incorporate them into our lives. If you do have each of these areas in place already, then take some time to pray about what God is calling you to do right now. What areas you need to strengthen. He wants to speak to you. He desires to make you the most incredible man or woman of God you can possibly be . . . and eventually the best husband or wife possible.

In Closing

A few years ago I sat on a long flight beside a girl who was raised in a very religious home. She shared with me that she was now a professional orchestral musician and it was her love of music that drew her away from "the church" (as in her religion it was frowned up to perform publicly). She spoke about how she connects with God through music and not any form of religion. As she shared, I then shared about my life, and how God had changed me. I spoke about the Lord as the very personal God He is, and I explained how it seems like my life gets clearer and more exciting the more I get to know Him. I'll never forget her response to me. "I've never heard anyone talk about God like you do. You're giving me a lot to think about," she said. I would have loved to have prayed with her right there, but I felt like my job that day was just to share what I did. What stuck with me though was that there she was, a person who had been around people who knew "about" God. She knew people who were called Christians, and yet she'd never heard someone talk about Him in real, practical personal terms that impacted their everyday life. My heart was so sad to think, 'Where are all the Believers? Where are the people who live this life, not as a religion, but as a part of everything they do? Why aren't people hearing about You the way You really are Lord?' Whatever the answers are, I want to exhort you that today is a new day for you and the Lord. In fact, your life is just beginning. I don't care how old you are. **You can BE the proof to this world.** To be able to emphatically share about God and who He really is, not because you've heard about Him, but because you actually know Him. Marriage, career, calling . . . expect more than what's typical. Expect His best.

Nothing will ever again be more important to you than the joy of living for the Lord.

A Single's Scripture Meditation List

1) Believing God Has Only Good In Store For You

    a. *"For I know the thoughts that I think toward you, says the Lord, thoughts of peace and not of evil, to give you a future and a hope. Then you will call upon Me and go and pray to Me, and I will listen to you. And you will seek Me and find Me, when you search for Me with all your heart. I will be found by you, says the Lord . . ."*
       (Jeremiah 29:11–14a)

    b. *"Every good gift and every perfect gift is from above, and comes down from the Father of lights, with whom there is no variation or shadow of turning."*
       (James 1:7)

    c. *"The Lord is my shepherd; I shall not want. He makes me to lie down in green pastures; He leads me beside the still waters. He restores my soul; He leads me in the paths of righteousness for His name's sake . . ."*
       (Psalm 23:1–3)

2) Repenting From Living Outside of God's Will

    a. *"Create in me a clean heart, O God, and renew a steadfast spirit within me." (Psalm 51:10)*

    b. *"For He who would love life and see good days, let him refrain his tongue from evil, and his lips from speaking* deceit. Let him turn away from evil and do good; let him seek peace and pursue it. For the eyes of the Lord are on the righteous, and His ears are open to their prayers" (1 Peter 3:10–12a)

c. "If we confess our sins, He is faithful and just to forgive us our sins and to cleanse us from all unrighteousness." (1 John 1:9)

d. "And you, being dead in your trespasses and the uncircumcision of your flesh, He has made alive together with Him, having forgiven you all trespasses, having wiped out the handwriting of requirements that was against us, which was contrary to us. And He has taken it out of the way, having nailed it to the cross." (Colossians 2:13, 14)

3) Releasing Forgiveness

a. "And whenever you stand praying, if you have anything against anyone, forgive him, that your Father in heaven may also forgive you your trespasses." (Mark 11:25)

b. "And forgive us our debts, as we forgive our debtors." (Matthew 6:12)

c. "Then Peter came to Him and said, "Lord, how often shall my brother sin against me, and I forgive him? Up to seven times?" Jesus said to him, "I do not say to you, up to seven times, but up to seventy times seven." (Matthew 18:21, 22)

4) Having Faith and Patience

a. ". . . that you do not become sluggish, but imitate those who through faith and patience inherit the promises." (Hebrews 6:12)

b. "And so, after he had patiently endured, he obtained the promise." (Hebrews 6:15)

c. "And let us not grow weary while doing good, for in due season we shall reap if we do not lose heart." (Galatians 6:9)

5) Trusting For the Right Spouse

a. "He who finds a wife finds a good thing and obtains favor from the Lord." (Proverbs 18:22)

b. *"... no good thing will He withhold from those who walk uprightly." (Psalm 87:11b)*

c. *"Delight yourself also in the LORD, and He shall give you the desires of your heart." (Psalm 37:4)*

d. *"So I say to you, ask, and it will be given to you; seek, and you will find; knock, and it will be opened to you." (Luke 11:9)*

About the Author

*T*ammy was raised in a Christian home in Alberta, Canada. Her first leadership role was as a Sunday school teacher at the age of 12. Since then, she has continued to serve as a leader and a teacher of God's Word.

While attending LIFE Bible College (now Life Pacific College) she began to volunteer as part of a start-up church in Anaheim, California. Now a large and growing congregation, The Rock, Anaheim Foursquare Church, is where Tammy serves as an Associate Pastor. It was there in 2007 that she first shared *"Single—for Now,"* a seminar calling singles to pursue and enjoy God's calling regardless of marital status.

Tammy is an ordained minister with the Foursquare Church and also serves as the Event Manager in their Central Offices in Los Angeles, California. Known as a passionate and expressive speaker, this is Tammy's first book.

**For audio messages, blogs and more,
visit tammysevcov.com.**

CPSIA information can be obtained at www.ICGtesting.com
Printed in the USA
BVOW012027080713

325394BV00002B/2/P